Key Topics in Coaching Psychology

Offering a concise and easy-to-read introduction to the subject, this book deals with key topics in the study of coaching psychology. It explains what coaching psychology is, when and why it is used, and what research can tell us about how and why it works.

The book opens with an exploration of the key foundations of coaching psychology, including how it is defined, where it began, and how has it developed. This is followed by an overview of the key theories informing coaching psychology: person-centred theories, goal-setting theory, adult learning theory, and the main theoretical approaches to coaching (behavioural coaching, cognitive behavioural coaching, psychodynamic coaching, and systemic coaching). The authors discuss the key methodologies used in coaching psychology research, covering both quantitative and qualitative approaches, before exploring the impact of coaching psychology on five areas of practice: coaching in the workplace, career coaching, coaching in education, life coaching, and health coaching. Finally, they suggest future directions for the field by examining emerging areas in research and practice.

Academically informed, and fully integrating key theories with application in coaching practice, this book gives readers a comprehensive yet accessible understanding of coaching psychology. *Key Topics in Coaching Psychology* is the ideal resource for undergraduate and postgraduate students of coaching psychology and occupational psychology, business, and leadership, as well as anyone with an interest in learning more about coaching psychology.

Rebecca J. Jones is a Professor of Coaching and Behaviour Change, and the Director of the Henley Centre for Coaching at Henley Business School, UK, where she leads the coaching faculty who are responsible for teaching the next generation of coaching practitioners. She is a chartered psychologist and co-founder of the Inclusive Leadership Company.

Holly Andrews has worked in academia for more than 15 years and is an Associate Professor in Coaching and Behaviour Change at Henley Business School, UK. She is Programme Director for the Henley MSc in Coaching for Behavioural Change, which provides some of the most in-depth coach education in the world.

BPS Key Topics Series
British Psychological Society

Routledge, in partnership with the British Psychological Society (BPS), is pleased to present *BPS Key Topics in Psychology*, a series of short introductory books that focus on a specific field within psychology. Each book is broken down into bitesize chunks to provide a helpful overview of core psychology topics, made clear by a five-part structure: foundations, theories, methodologies, impacts, and emerging areas. Written by active and experienced authors, these essential books encourage students to approach fundamental concepts with confidence and critical thinking.

Books may incorporate student-friendly pedagogies, including tools such as: feature boxes; key terms and definitions; and links to further reading online. Concise yet comprehensive, these books offer a simple and accessible overview of core psychology topics for students looking for a summary of key concepts in the topic, or those new to the area.

For more information about this series, please visit: www.routledge.com/bps-key-topics/book-series/BPSKT

Key Topics in Quantitative Research
Paul Christiansen

Key Topics in Coaching Psychology
Rebecca J. Jones and Holly Andrews

Key Topics in Coaching Psychology

Rebecca J. Jones and
Holly Andrews

Routledge
Taylor & Francis Group

LONDON AND NEW YORK

Designed cover image: Getty Images @artisteer

First published 2026
by Routledge
4 Park Square, Milton Park, Abingdon, Oxon OX14 4RN

and by Routledge
605 Third Avenue, New York, NY 10158

Routledge is an imprint of the Taylor & Francis Group, an informa business

© 2026 Rebecca J. Jones and Holly Andrews

British Library Cataloguing-in-Publication Data
A catalogue record for this book is available from the British Library

ISBN: 9781032686431 (hbk)
ISBN: 9781032686387 (pbk)
ISBN: 9781032686448 (ebk)

DOI: 10.4324/9781032686448

Typeset in Galliard
by Newgen Publishing UK

Access the Support Material: www.routledge.com/9781032686431

The joy of being a coach educator is that you get to work with incredible coaches. This book is dedicated to the amazing team in the coaching group at Henley Business School and the fantastic work they do.

Contents

Section 1

Key Foundations

This section in summary

- Coaching is a learning and development tool with the goal of producing behavioural change.
- Definitions of coaching lack precision, often with high levels of ambiguity and little to distinguish coaching from other similar interventions.
- In a bid to advance the profession of coaching, several professional bodies have been established. However, unlike many other professions, there is no single accepted professional body.
- The key difference between coaching and coaching psychology is the qualification and training received by the coach (i.e., a coaching psychologist is a qualified coach and psychologist, whereas other coaches may not have the background training in psychology).
- References to coaching appear from the early 1900s, but coaching as we know it came into the mainstream towards the end of the twentieth century.
- Key figures in the development of coaching are Sir John Whitmore, who introduced the GROW model of coaching, and Laura Whitworth and Thomas Leonard, who developed the Co-Active coaching movement.

DOI: 10.4324/9781032686448-1

- Coaching psychology developed from 1960s therapeutic traditions but comes to the fore at the turn of the twenty-first century.
- Anthony Grant and Stephen Palmer are key figures in the development of coaching psychology, being involved with developing coaching psychology courses and professional bodies.
- The need to develop an evidence base to distinguish coaching as a discipline in its own right has been a driving force in the development of coaching psychology.
- The rise of positive psychology furthered the development of coaching psychology, providing suitable underpinning theories and frameworks to explain the impact of coaching.
- The professionalisation of coaching has led to the development of coaching psychology professional bodies, which set out clear standards for the practice of coaching psychology.
- The need to train coaches in a rigorous way has also contributed to the development of coaching psychology, as students of coaching need to understand the psychological theories that underpin the practice of coaching.

Chapter 1

What Is Coaching Psychology?

What is coaching?

Coaching is a learning and development tool with the goal of producing behavioural change (Jones, 2021). **Coaches** achieve this goal by asking **coachees open questions**, listening, and using tools and techniques to enable coachees to **reflect** and to raise their awareness of how to overcome the challenges they are facing. Coaching is normally conducted on a one-to-one basis, however there are also other forms of coaching, such as **team coaching** (where a whole team is coached) or **group coaching** (where a group of individuals come together to be coached).

Coaching. A learning and development tool with the goal of producing behavioural change.
Coach. Someone who provides coaching.
Coachee. Someone who receives coaching.
Open question. A question that requires a more detailed response (e.g., How do you feel about working here?).
Reflect. To think deeply or carefully about something.
Team coaching. Coaching provided to an intact team (i.e., a group of people who have a shared goal).
Group coaching. Where a group of individuals come together to be coached.

DOI: 10.4324/9781032686448-2

Academic perspective to defining coaching

There have been various definitions offered by academics writing on the topic of coaching. Greif and colleagues (2022) provide a review of the definitions of coaching, highlighting how, in many cases, the definitions offered are not precise, often having high levels of ambiguity and little to distinguish coaching from other similar interventions.

One definition that offers some degree of precision is provided by Bono and colleagues (2009) who state that coaching is a one-to-one learning and development **intervention** that uses a collaborative, reflective, goal-focused relationship to achieve professional outcomes that are valued by the coachee, often focusing on **interpersonal** and **intrapersonal** issues.

> **Intervention**. A structured programme or activity.
> **Interpersonal**. The relationship between individuals.
> **Intrapersonal**. The internal processes within an individual.

Helpfully, this definition describes the outcomes of coaching (learning and development focused on interpersonal and intrapersonal issues; professional outcomes valued by the coachee) and how coaching achieves this (one-to-one, collaborative, reflective, goal-focused relationship). Implicit in this definition is that coaching is a work-based intervention as the desired outcome are "professional outcomes", however it is likely that removing "professional" in this definition would make it equally applicable to other forms of coaching such as health coaching, where outcomes will be health-related, or life coaching where outcomes could link to any aspect of the coachee's life.

Practitioner perspective to defining coaching

The profession of coaching is often described as **unregulated**, with no real barriers to entry: anyone can call themselves a "coach". Therefore, in a bid to advance the profession of coaching by setting standards and providing **certification**, a number of coaching professional bodies have been established. However, unlike many other professions, there is no single accepted **professional body**. In the UK, there are three "main" professional bodies that the majority of practicing coaches tend to become a member of. These are the International Coach Federation (ICF), the European Mentoring and Coaching Council (EMCC) and the Association for Coaching (AC). Each of these professional bodies provide their own definition of coaching and their own route to **accreditation** so that coaches can advertise themselves as an ICF/EMCC/AC accredited coach.

Unregulated. Not subject to formal rules or control of an authority or governing body.

Certification. Formal recognition of meeting specific standards or competencies.

Professional bodies. Organisations that represent, support, and regulate those working in a particular profession, such as coaching. Coaching professional bodies include the International Coach Federation (ICF), European Mentoring and Coaching Council (EMCC), and Association for Coaching (AC).

Accreditation. Formal process where an authoritative body, such as a professional body, grants official recognition based on meeting specific standards or competencies.

For example, the ICF defines coaching as "partnering with coachees in a thought-provoking and creative process that inspires them to maximize their personal and professional potential. The process of coaching often unlocks previously untapped sources of imagination, productivity and leadership" (ICF, 2023). Whereas the AC defines coaching as "a facilitated, dialogic and reflective learning process that aims to grow the individual[']s (or team[']s) awareness, responsibility and choice (thinking and behavioural)" (Association for Coaching, 2023).

Interestingly, the essence of each of these two definitions feels quite different. On the one hand, the ICF emphasises the creative aspect of coaching, using words such as creative, thought-provoking, and imagination, a definition that Greif and colleagues (2022) critically describe as a persuasive definition, aimed at selling coaching. On the other hand, the definition offered by the AC feels more aligned with the academic definition provided by Bono and colleagues (2009) in that both emphasise the learning and reflective elements of coaching.

Box 1.1   Do definitions matter?

The differences in the definitions of coaching can raise some interesting questions for us to consider.

- What is the purpose of a definition?
- Who or what audience is the definition for?
- How can a clear definition be useful from the different perspectives of a researcher, the coach, the coachee, the profession as a whole?
- How might these different styles of definition serve each of these purposes?

How is coaching similar to and different from other interventions?

Given the absence of an agreed definition, either from the academic or practitioner perspectives, it can be helpful to draw comparisons with other forms of learning and development or one-to-one interventions, to highlight the similarities and differences across these interventions. Coaching, **mentoring** and **counselling** are often considered "helping" relationships and conducted on a

Mentoring. A developmental relationship in which a more experienced mentor provides developmental support to a less experienced mentee.

one-to-one basis; and coaching, mentoring and **training** are usually (but not always) used in professional contexts and aimed at professional development. Table 1.1 outlines the distinctions between coaching, training, mentoring, and counselling.

Therefore, to help us to understand what coaching is, we can consider how it is similar to and different from other interventions. Specifically, we can consider the practitioner's expertise, the nature of the relationship, whether the practitioner gives advice and how they handle questions when asked, who leads the interaction, and the duration and focus of the intervention. As illustrated in Table 1.1, there is a high degree of overlap between many of the interventions. However, it is perhaps the combination of these functions that helps us to distinguish coaching as a learning and development tool.

Counselling. A therapeutic process in which a trained counsellor provides support to manage personal, emotional, psychological, or behavioural challenges.

Training. The process of teaching or developing specific skills, knowledge, or competencies.

What is coaching psychology?

The British Psychological Society (BPS) defines **coaching psychology** as "the scientific study and application of behaviour, cognition and emotion to deepen our understanding of individuals' and groups' performance, achievement and wellbeing, and to enhance practice within coaching" (British Psychological Society, 2023).

Coaching psychology. The scientific study and application of behaviour, cognition, and emotion to deepen our understanding of individuals' and groups' performance, achievement, and wellbeing, and to enhance practice within coaching.

Table 1.1 Comparison of coaching, teaching, mentoring, and counselling

Function	Coaching	Teaching	Mentoring	Counselling
Expertise	Generic helping expertise that can be applied to different contexts. High level of skills in questioning and reflecting.	Subject-specific expertise. High level of knowledge in their area of expertise.	Subject- or profession-specific expertise. High level of knowledge in their area of expertise.	Helping expertise that can be applied to explore trauma or difficult situations, thoughts, and emotions. High level of skills in questioning and reflecting.
Relationship	Depends upon creating a sharing, trusting relationship.	Relationship of different status between teacher and student.	Relationship of different status between mentor and mentee, although also requires a trusting relationship.	Depends upon creating a sharing trusting relationship.
Advice Approach to answering questions	Avoids giving advice. Maintains a belief that people can find their own solutions.	Gives advice. Offers solutions from their own "expert" position.	Gives advice. Offers solutions from their own "expert" position.	Avoids giving advice. Maintains a belief that people can find their own solutions.

Led by	Coachee has ownership of change and development and dictates the focus of the session.	Teacher gives guidance on the focus by dictating what needs to be learnt.	Mentee usually suggests topics to explore however, will be guided by what the mentor recommends is important.	Counsellor dictates the direction of the discussion.
Duration	Relationship generally has a set duration.	Relationship generally has a set duration.	Ongoing relationship that can last for a long time.	Relationship duration can vary however can last for a long time.
Focus	Focuses on the whole person in the context of goal pursuit.	Focuses on specific subject knowledge and skills.	Focuses on career and personal development.	Tends to focus predominately on the past and relationships.

Whybrow and Palmer (2019) highlight that, when comparing coaching psychology as defined by psychological professional bodies and coaching as defined by professional bodies, the difference is that coaching psychologists are more likely to include psychology or psychological approaches in the coaching tools, techniques, and approaches that they engage in. However, the reality is that most coaching education programmes, even those described as coaching rather than coaching psychology, tend to be informed by principles drawn from psychological theory, research, and practice – goal-setting being a classic example of this. Given that psychology is the study of the human mind and how it influences behaviour, and the purpose of coaching is behaviour change, it is not surprising that most of coaching practice has been informed, to some extent, by psychology.

Box 1.2   Coaching or coaching psychology?

Most approaches to coaching are informed in some way or another by psychological theories (even if this is implicit or historical). Therefore, there is often very little to distinguish between coaching and coaching psychology. Passmore and colleagues (2016) suggest that one approach to defining coaching psychology is to consider it as the *study of coaching practice* as opposed to a distinctive aspect of coaching practice itself. For many practitioners, the key difference may be the qualification and training received by the coach (i.e., a coaching psychologist is a qualified coach and psychologist, whereas other coaches may not have the background training in psychology). The debate regarding whether it is necessary for coaches to also be psychologists has been running for many years now. For example, a study by Bono and colleagues in 2009 compared the practices of executive coaches who were also psychologists with those who were not, with their main conclusion being that differences between coaches who were psychologists and those who were non-psychologist coaches were generally quite small. However, more recently, Bozer and colleagues (2014) found that when coaches have a background in psychology, their

---

coaching led to increased self-awareness in coachees. As with many areas of coaching psychology, this is an area where more data is needed before we can draw firm conclusions on the importance in coaching of a background in psychology.

You will find that beyond this chapter, in the rest of the book, we will often use the terms "coaching" and "coaching psychology" interchangeably.

How is coaching psychology used in practice?

Coaching psychology can be considered a **multidisciplinary** approach to behavioural change, drawing on decades of research in the disciplines of psychology and leadership to inform the tools, techniques, and practices used by coaching psychologists. The application of coaching psychology is, in most respects, very similar if not the

Multidisciplinary. An approach that involves the integration of knowledge and perspectives from different fields of study.

same as the application of coaching. As highlighted earlier, the key differentiator is the background training of the coach. Coaching psychology has been applied to almost every domain where behaviour change is required, many of which will be explored in further detail in Section 4 of this book.

The largest area of the practice of coaching psychology is in the workplace. Coaching psychology can be used very broadly to support individuals' goal attainment as part of a "perk" for high-performing individuals to further advance their career or to support those who are under-performing and need some additional support to get them back on track. Coaching psychology can also be used to enhance or complement other forms of learning and development – for example, a series of coaching sessions might accompany a formal training programme, particularly leadership development. Coaching can also be used to support transitions – for example, when someone has been promoted to a new role, when they are retiring, or when they are returning to work after a period of parental leave.

In addition to coaching in the workplace, coaching can also be used by individuals to support them with broader life goals – for example, individuals might seek a life coach who can work with them in relation to goals that are not isolated to one domain of their life, such as work, and instead might touch on goals related to multiple aspects of their life, such as romantic relationships, family, health, and work. Health coaching on the other hand is specifically focused on supporting individuals with health-related goals, such as losing weight or getting fit.

When we think of coaching psychology, we can consider that theories and research from psychology inform multiple aspects of coaching. For example, how the coach behaves, how the coach thinks and feels about their coachee, and the things that the coach does. Section 2 of this book will explore the influence of psychological theories in these areas in greater detail. Psychology has helped us to understand why individuals might struggle to change their behaviour or achieve their goals and coaching is one way in which we can apply this learning to support individuals to overcome these challenges.

Aim of the book and overview of contents

The aim of this book is to provide readers with a simple, yet broad, overview of core topics in coaching psychology, all presented in bite-size chunks. This text provides the reader with a comprehensive yet easy-to-digest understanding of coaching psychology and is an ideal introductory text for psychology and business students as well as anyone with an interest in learning more about coaching psychology.

In Chapter 2, we explore the origins of coaching psychology, including the founding figures in coaching and coaching psychology, with a focus on how (and why) coaching psychology has developed.

Section 2 explores key theories of coaching psychology. It includes Chapter 3, which explores how person-centred theories, such as the concept of unconditional positive regard, have influenced how coaches think about their coachees, and how this can in turn influence coachee behaviour change. Chapter 4 explores goal-setting theory, including how coaches can use goal-setting theory to help coachees improve performance. Chapter 5's focus is on theories of adult learning that provide an explanatory mechanism for how coaching leads to learning and development. This includes the importance of a strong coaching relationship to facilitate reflection. Finally, for this section, Chapter 6 explores four of the main theoretical approaches to coaching: behavioural coaching, cognitive-behavioural coaching, psychodynamic coaching, and systemic coaching.

Section 3 focuses on key research methodologies in coaching psychology with Chapter 7 exploring how quantitative methodologies, including randomised control trials, surveys, and meta-analyses, are used within coaching research. This is followed by Chapter 8, which explores how qualitative methodologies, including interviews, observations, and systematic literature reviews, are used within coaching research.

Section 4 explores key impacts of coaching psychology on practice. In this section, Chapter nine is dedicated to the largest area of coaching practice: coaching at work. Chapter 10 focuses on career coaching, which is aimed at supporting people when they are making career choices. Chapter 11 is centred on coaching in education and explains how coaching can be used as a pedagogical approach to learning and teaching at all levels of education. Chapter 12 is about life coaching, which is often seen as the most controversial area of coaching practice. Finally, for this section, Chapter 13 discusses health coaching, which supports people to change aspects of their lifestyle.

The final section of this book, Section 5, discusses key emerging areas of coaching psychology. This section consists of Chapter 14, which outlines the key areas for future research in coaching psychology, and Chapter 15, which explores the current trends in coaching psychology practice, such as the application of artificial intelligence to coaching.

Further reading and resources

British Psychological Society. (2020, 7 July). *Coaching Psychology – A Day in the Life with Cornelia Lucey* [Video]. YouTube. https://youtu.be/VdzSi5QovN4.

The Coaching Crowd with Jo Wheatley & Zoe Hawkins. (2021, 10 November). The difference between coaching, mentoring and counselling (No. 001) [Audio podcast episode]. https://podcasts.apple.com/gb/podcast/001-the-difference-between-coaching-mentoring/id159 4603806?i=1000541338900.

WorkLifePsych TV. (2022, 6 January). *What Is Coaching? Insights from a Coaching Psychologist* [Video]. YouTube. https://www.youtube.com/watch?v=-2GBZ-PEEtY.

References

Association for Coaching. (2023). *Why Coaching?* https://www.associa tionforcoaching.com/page/WhyCoaching#:~:text=What%20is%20c oaching%3F,choice%20(thinking%20and%20behavioural). Retrieved 30 October 2023.

Bono, J. E., Purvanova, R. K., Towler, A. J., & Peterson, D. B. (2009). A survey of executive coaching practices. *Personnel Psychology, 62*(2), 361–404.

Bozer, G. C., Sarros, J., & C. Santora, J. (2014). Academic background and credibility in executive coaching effectiveness. *Personnel Review, 43*(6), 881–897.

British Psychological Society. (2023). Division of Coaching Psychology. https://www.bps.org.uk/member-networks/division-coaching-psy chology. Retrieved 30 October 2023.

Greif, S., Möller, H., Scholl, W., Passmore, J., & Müller, F. (2022). Coaching definitions and concepts. In S. Greif, H. Möller, W. Scholl, J. Passmore, & F. Müller (eds), *International Handbook of Evidence-Based Coaching: Theory, Research and Practice* (pp. 1–12). Springer International Publishing.

ICF (2023). *All Things Coaching.* Accessed from https://coachingfed eration.org/about#:~:text=ICF%20defines%20coaching%20as%20par tnering,of%20imagination%2C%20productivity%20and%20leadership. Retrieved 30 October 2023.

Jones, R. J. (2021). *Coaching with Research in Mind.* Routledge.

Passmore, J., Peterson, D. B., & Freire, T. (2016). The psychology of coaching and mentoring. In J. Passmore, D. B. Peterson, & T. Freire (eds), *The Psychology of Coaching and Mentoring.* Wiley Blackwell.

Whybrow, A., & Palmer, S. (2019). Past, present and future. In S. Palmer & A. Whybrow (eds), *Handbook of Coaching Psychology: A Guide for Practitioners* (2nd edition, pp. 5–13). Routledge.

Chapter 2

Where Did It Begin and How Has It Developed?

The origins of coaching psychology

As alluded to in Chapter 1, the distinction between coaching and coaching psychology is ill-defined and therefore the origin of coaching psychology is intertwined with the origin of coaching. Passmore and Lai (2021) found references to coaching in educational contexts as early as 1911 and references to coaching in business from the 1930s. Palmer and Whybrow (2017) identify that some of the earliest discussions of coaching psychology are in the domain of **sports coaching**. Coleman Griffith published a book in 1926 entitled *Psychology of Coaching*, focusing on aspects of sports coaching that benefit from an understanding of psychology, such as handling fame. Griffith is generally credited as founding modern-day sports psychology, but his contributions to coaching psychology are less well known (Whybrow & Palmer, 2019).

Coaching psychology as we know it today is seen as having developed from two main areas of counselling and **therapy**: the

> **Sports coaching.** An intervention to support athletes designed to improve their performance and skills in a specific sport.

> **Therapy.** An intervention aimed at supporting individuals intended to overcome emotional, psychological, or behavioural challenges.

DOI: 10.4324/9781032686448-3

humanistic tradition and the cognitive behavioural tradition (Palmer & Whybrow, 2008a). While both these approaches developed in the 1960s, they focused on very different psychological underpinnings. The humanistic tradition focuses on the quality of the rela-

> **Humanistic.** A psychological approach that emphasises the intrinsic worth and potential of individuals.
>
> **Cognitive-behavioural.** A psychological approach that emphasises the link between thoughts, emotions, and behaviour.

tionship between the helping professional and coachee, assuming that, given the right conditions, the coachee will develop naturally (see Chapter 3 for a discussion of person-centred coaching, which stems from the humanist tradition). In contrast, while the relationship between professional and coachee is important to cognitive behavioural professionals, their focus is on helping the coachee to uncover and change maladaptive thoughts (see Chapter 6 for a discussion of cognitive-behavioural approaches to coaching). The underpinning assumptions of both these approaches can still be seen in modern coaching psychology.

This chapter explores the history of coaching psychology to the present day and Chapter 15 explores the future of coaching psychology.

Founding figures in coaching

In addition to these influential traditions, which have shaped the discipline of coaching psychology as it is today, there are also several notable founding figures. These founding figures are individuals who have had a significant impact on the practice of coaching. One such key figure is Sir John Whitmore (1937–2017), who was influential in defining coaching and bringing it into the mainstream for both organisations and academics. A shift in coaching discourse occurred with the publication of his 1992 book, *Coaching for Performance*, which has sold more than 1 million copies and has been translated into more than 20 languages (Performance Consultants, 2024). Whitmore's work was heavily influenced by sports psychology, particularly Timothy Gallwey's *The Inner Game of Tennis* (1974). Whitmore defined coaching as "unlocking people's potential to maximise their own performance" (Whitmore, 2002, p. 8). The book introduced the now ubiquitous **GROW model** of coaching (see Chapter 6), which has become a cornerstone of most beginner coach

GROW model. A coaching framework that leads the coachee through exploring their goals, current reality, options, and way forward.

education. His impact on the coaching industry was, and continues to be, significant. He was a key part of the International Coach Federation (ICF), European Mentoring and Coaching Council (EMCC), and Professional and Personal Coaches Association (PPCA), and he received numerous accolades from industry bodies such as these (Performance Consultants, 2024).

In the USA, Laura Whitworth and Thomas Leonard were equally influential in steering the direction of the coaching profession. While their relationship could be described as turbulent (Brock, 2009), they collaborated in setting up the Co-Active Training Institute (formerly The Coaches Training Institute) in 1992 (Co-Active Training Institute, 2024). The Co-Active methodology focuses on finding meaning in life via communication and connection with others and taking action from our "being" rather than focusing on "doing" (Kimsey-House et al., 2018). While Whitworth stayed with the Co-Active coaching movement, Leonard took his work in a different direction, founding Coach U also in 1992 (Coach U, n.d.). Coach U is considered one of the first coaching training schools in the world and it is where Leonard founded the ICF (Coach U, n.d.). Leonard is credited with popularising coaching, using his media know-how to gain publicity for the profession (Brock, 2009).

Founding figures in coaching psychology

In addition to these founding figures for coaching more generally, when we consider coaching psychology specifically there are two key founding figures who have been highly influential.

Professor Anthony Grant (1954–2020) is widely regarded as a key figure in the establishment of coaching psychology (Institute of Coaching, n.d.). Grant studied psychology before embarking upon a career as an academic and practitioner in coaching. In 2000 he set up the world's first ever academic Coaching Psychology Unit at the University of Sydney and as director of the unit he was involved in the development and delivery of coaching psychology courses. Grant had a vast back-catalogue of publications, collaborating with researchers worldwide to contribute to the development of **evidence-based coaching** (Sorensen, 2022). Grant is credited with running the first **randomised control trial** in coaching (see Chapter 7 for more on randomised control trials), a key milestone in providing an evidence-base for the efficacy of coaching (Sorensen, 2022). Grant applied the discipline of psychology to coaching, seeking to provide a theoretical framework and evidence-based principles for applied practice (Grant, 2006).

Evidence-based coaching. A coaching approach that is underpinned by theory and research.
Randomised control trial. A research design where participants are randomly allocated to different research conditions that involve receiving an intervention (or not).

Professor Stephen Palmer is another influential figure in the development of coaching psychology as a discipline. Palmer has been particularly involved with the British Psychological Society's (BPS) recognition of coaching psychology as a branch of applied psychology. He set up the BPS Special Interest Group in Coaching Psychology in 2004, which developed into the Division of Coaching Psychology (see below for more details on the development of the BPS Division of Coaching Psychology). He is also the president and a fellow of the International Society for Coaching Psychology (Centre for Coaching, 2024). Like Grant, Palmer is heavily involved in advancing coaching psychology via research. He has published over 60 books including one of the first texts dedicated to coaching psychology, *Handbook of Coaching Psychology* (Palmer & Whybrow, 2008b), and is consulting editor of the *International Journal of Coaching Psychology* (Centre for Coaching, 2024).

How and why has coaching psychology developed?

The turn of the twentieth century marks a key point in the development of coaching psychology. Grant (2005) examined the volume of published literature on coaching psychology and found a marked rise in publications from 1995 onwards. There are four probable factors involved in the increased interest in coaching psychology at this point. The first is the need to develop a body of knowledge that those practising coaching can draw upon. Second, the rise of the **positive psychology** movement occurred at about the same time and provided a suitable underpinning theory for the discipline of coaching. Third, there was an increased focus on the professionalisation of coaching and coaching psychology at about this time, with the creation of professional groups, standards, and a focus on evidence-based practice (Whybrow & Palmer, 2019). Finally, the need to train people to be effective coaches also became increasingly important in this period.

> **Positive psychology.** A psychological approach that emphasises positive aspects of human experience, such as happiness and flourishing.

Evidence in coaching

Coaching practice itself developed at a greater rate than research and evidence about coaching (Jones, 2021). Much of the original work on coaching, while often based on psychological principles, did not explicitly refer to these principles and consequently was then used and developed in an atheoretical way (Linley & Harrington, 2008). Research is required to delineate coaching from other helping professions and provide a robust evidence base regarding what works and for whom (Fillery-Travis & Corrie, 2019). Coaching psychology, with its focus on the rigorous application of methodologies from psychology, has been ideally placed to fill this gap in coaching knowledge.

Fillery-Travis & Corrie (2019) outline six benefits of taking an evidence-based approach to coaching:

1 Coaches can ensure that the interventions they deliver are those most likely to deliver the results desired by the coachee.
2 Coaches keep their knowledge up to date and make decisions based on this contemporary knowledge.
3 Standards are maintained, ensuring more consistent results for coachees.
4 Confidence in coaching services increase, both in coaches and in buyers of coaching.
5 The choice to apply coaching techniques can be based on more rigorous evidence than personal experience and intuition.
6 It provides an ethical basis for taking people's money in return for services.

The development of coaching psychology has coincided with, and may be responsible for, a rapid increase in the volume of literature published on coaching, each piece addressing to a greater or lesser extent the desire for coaching to be able to claim that it is an evidence-based profession (Grant, 2005). However, there are questions over the quality of the evidence available (Jones, 2021) and whether it meets the needs of practicing coaches and coaching psychologists (Fillery-Travis & Corrie, 2019). Consequently, there remain calls for greater research into coaching, including the outcomes of coaching and how impactful results are obtained (Bozer & Jones, 2018).

Box 2.1 What is "good" evidence?

What makes "good" evidence is not clear-cut. Fillery-Travis and Corrie (2019) call for coaching researchers and practitioners to take a critical view of the notion of evidence. Following the traditions of other evidence-based practice professions such as healthcare, rigorous studies with large sample sizes utilising scientific approaches to data collection and analysis are prized as the highest form of evidence. However, these studies often do not connect with coaches, who instead are looking for a deeper understanding of individual cases and something that resonates with their personal experience. Considering what kind of evidence is needed in coaching psychology offers an opportunity to create an evidence base that provides not only what is traditionally considered as good evidence, but what actually works for coaching psychologists. Chapters 7 and 8 consider research methodologies in coaching psychology in more detail.

Coaching psychology and positive psychology

Positive psychology "focuses on scientific inquiry into positive aspects of human experience and the application of this knowledge in a broad range of clinical and non-clinical contexts" (Carr, 2022, p. 25). The positive psychology movement started as a response to the dominant tradition in psychology of working to alleviate mental ill health or negative experiences in people, with little attention being paid to helping people move from having an absence of negative symptoms to positive experiences such as happiness, engagement, and flourishing. Martin Seligman's (2002) work on happiness and Mihaly Cziksentmihalyi's (1990) work on flow are crucial foundations for the positive psychology movement. Key topics and theories in positive psychology centre around concepts such as wellbeing, happiness, flow, strengths, hope, optimism, mindfulness, and flourishing (Panchal et al., 2019).

Smith and colleagues (2021) identify that there is an intimate relationship between positive psychology, as the science of human flourishing, and coaching, as the pathway to human thriving. In their book *Positive Psychology Coaching in the Workplace*, the authors identify a large and consistent body of research linking positive emotions, traits, and states in employees (such as satisfaction, wellbeing, happiness, and engagement) with positive outcomes for employers (such as increased productivity and lower absence and turnover rates). Such evidence helps to provide the impetus for greater understanding of how we can promote such states in employees through processes such as coaching.

Positive psychology can provide much of the scientific underpinning and research that coaching psychology can be seen to lack, helping to validate what coaching psychologists do (Linley & Harrington, 2008). In practice, many coaching psychologists use positive psychology as the underpinning model for their coaching, with this approach being selected more than any other in a survey of international coaching practices (Palmer & Whybrow, 2017).

The close linkages between positive psychology and coaching psychology have led to the development of **positive psychology coaching (PPC)**. PPC can be defined as "evidence-based coaching practice informed by the theories and research

> **Positive psychology coaching (PPC).** Evidence-based coaching practice informed by the theories and research of positive psychology for the enhancement of resilience, achievement, and wellbeing.

of positive psychology for the enhancement of resilience, achievement and well-being" (Green & Palmer, 2014 cited in Green & Palmer, 2019). There are specific tools that have been developed for use within PPC (Panchal et al., 2019). These include the three good things exercise, where coachees are tasked with writing down three good things that have occurred every day, and using strengths in a new way, where coachees identify their top strengths and try to use them in a different way every day for a week (see Panchal et al., 2019).

Professionalisation of coaching and coaching psychology

As the practice of coaching has grown, so have calls to increase the professionalisation and regulation of the coaching profession. Once referred to as the "wild west" (Sherman & Freas, 2004), coaching now has a number of professional bodies that seek to provide guidance on standards, ethics, and the ongoing development of the discipline (see Chapter 1 for a discussion of the main coaching professional bodies). This drive for professionalisation means that stakeholders are also seeking to understand the theory behind coaching and see robust evidence regarding its efficacy.

Despite coaching having several professional bodies, there was no unified voice integrating psychological theory and evidence with the practice of coaching before the development of professional bodies explicitly governing coaching psychology (Palmer & Whybrow, 2005). Professional bodies for coaching psychology have developed to steer those who consider themselves to be coaching psychologists. In the UK, this started with the British Psychological Society Coaching Psychology Forum (CPF), which was founded in 2002 as an internet-based forum. Members of the CPF petitioned for the BPS to set up a special interest group to support those psychologists who were practising as coaches. The BPS Special Interest Group in Coaching Psychology (SGCP) was consequently created in 2004. The mission of the SGCP was "to promote the development of coaching psychology at an academic and practitioner level, to develop ethical standards, and to foster a voice for psychology within the broader coaching arena" (Palmer & Whybrow, 2005, p. 5).

The SGCP continued up until 2021, when the group gained full divisional status within the BPS. The BPS Division of Coaching Psychology (DoCP) "supports psychologists, coaches, individuals and organisations who are interested in coaching psychology and coaching services. We share research and evidence-based insights that relate to the psychology of coaching" (British Psychological Society, 2024). With this redesignation as a division, there came pathways to becoming a **chartered coaching psychologist**, with accredited Master's level programmes launching at various UK universities in 2024 and a doctoral level BPS qualification in coaching psychology available for those wishing to become chartered. Support is provided to members via mechanisms such as peer practice groups, where members can

> **Chartered coaching psychologist.** A coaching psychologist who has achieved chartered status with the British Psychological Society by evidencing the required level of education and competence.

share their experiences of using psychology in their coaching practice. Members of the public are also supported in finding a suitably qualified and experienced coach via the Register of Coaching Psychologists (British Psychological Society, 2024).

Chartered coaching psychologists must demonstrate the standards set out by the DoCP as follows (British Psychological Society, 2024):

- Be effective, reflective, ethically sound, resourceful and informed practitioners able to work in a variety of contexts with a variety of individual, group and organisational coachees.
- Be able to make informed, autonomous judgements on complex issues, often in unpredictable environments and in the absence of complete data.
- Embody the creative, interpretive, personal and innovative aspects of coaching psychology, including detailed understanding of applicable perspectives and techniques for research and advanced academic enquiry.
- Demonstrate and commit to ongoing personal and professional development and inquiry, contributing substantially to the development of new techniques, ideas or approaches.
- Understand, develop and apply models of psychological inquiry for the creation and interpretation of new knowledge and professional practice of a quality to satisfy peer review, extend the forefront of the discipline and merit publication.
- Appreciate the significance of the wider social, cultural and political domains in which coaching psychologists operate.

- Adopt a questioning and evaluative approach to the philosophy, practice, research and theory that constitutes coaching psychology.

Internationally, other professional membership bodies have been established to serve coaching psychologists across the globe, notably the International Society for Coaching Psychology (ISCP). The ISCP aims to develop the discipline and profession of coaching psychology by encouraging theory, research, and practice in the area (ISCP, 2023). The society supports coaching psychology in various ways. For example, they run an annual International Congress of Coaching Psychology, bringing together the global coaching psychology community, engaging the psychology community and other professionals in coaching and coaching psychology, and promoting the development of coaching psychology across the world (Whybrow and Palmer, 2019). They accredit coaching psychologists and coach training courses, publish the *Journal Coaching Psychology International* and have a research centre fostering international collaboration on coaching psychology research (ISCP, 2023).

Coach training

As demand for coaching increases, so does the demand for coach training (see Chapter 15 for a discussion of the future of coach education). The ICF (2023) Global Coaching Study estimates there are more than 109,000 coach practitioners operating worldwide, and 85 per cent of these hold some kind of coaching credential or certification from a coach education organisation. These qualifications vary widely, from courses of a few hours to full Master's programmes and doctoral degrees in coaching. Coaches come into the profession from a huge variety of backgrounds, many with little or no knowledge of psychology. Many commercial coach training courses are based on proprietary models of coaching, with little theoretical underpinning. If they are based on theory, there is often no explicit discussion of the psychological principles of behavioural change that underpin the coaching (Grant, 2006). Consequently, some authors have asserted that inappropriately trained coaches take an atheoretical approach to their practice, using models that may not be suitable for the coachee or for the presenting issue and may even cause damage to the coachee (Grant, 2006).

While there is an attempt to provide credibility for standards for the coach training industry via professional body accreditation, there is still a desire for greater regulation and control of coach training. Psychology entering the coaching market has raised standards in coach education, with Grant (2006) highlighting that the focus of coaching psychology on rigorous training programmes, ethical practice, and qualifications has raised the bar in coach education.

Further reading and resources

British Psychological Society. (2024). Division of Coaching Psychology. https://www.bps.org.uk/member-networks/division-coaching-psychology.

ISCP. (2023). About the International Society for Coaching Psychology. https://www.isfcp.info/.

Zhou, L. (2024). *The Coaching Industry Market Size in 2024*. https://www.luisazhou.com/blog/coaching-industry-market-size. Retrieved 4 June 2024.

References

Bozer, G., & Jones, R. J. (2018). Understanding the factors that determine workplace coaching effectiveness: A systematic literature review. *European Journal of Work and Organizational Psychology*, *27*(3), 342–361.

British Psychological Society. (2024). Division of Coaching Psychology. https://www.bps.org.uk/member-networks/division-coaching-psychology.

Brock, V. (2009). Professional challenges facing the coaching field from an historical perspective. *International Journal of Coaching in Organizations*, *7*(1), 27–37.

Carr, A. (2022). *Positive Psychology: The Science of Wellbeing and Human Strengths* (3rd edition). Routledge.

Centre for Coaching (2024). Meet the team. https://www.centreforcoaching.com/our_team.

Co-Active Training Institute. (2024). About Us. https://coactive.com/about/.

Coach U (n.d.) Coach U. https://www.coachu.com/home/. Retrieved 16 October 2024.

Cziksentmihalyi, M. (1990). *Flow: The Psychology of Optimal Experience.* Harper and Row.

Fillery-Travis, A., & Collie, S. (2019). Research and the practitioner: Getting a perspective on coaching psychology research. In S. Palmer & A. Whybrow (eds), *Handbook of Coaching Psychology: A Guide for Practitioners* (2nd edition). Routledge.

Gallwey, T. W. (1974). *The Inner Game of Tennis.* Random House.

Grant, A. M. (2005). Workplace, executive and life coaching: An annotated bibliography from the behavioural science literature. Unpublished paper, University of Sydney, Coaching Psychology Unit.

Grant, A. M. (2006). A personal perspective on professional coaching and the development of coaching psychology. *International Coaching Psychology Review, 1*(1), 12–22.

Green, S., & Palmer, S. (2019). Positive psychology coaching: Science into practice. In S. Green & S. Palmer (eds), *Positive Psychology Coaching in Practice* (pp. 1–20). Routledge.

Griffith, C. R. (1926). *Psychology of Coaching: A Study of Coaching Methods from the Point of View of Psychology.* Charles Scribner's Sons.

ICF (2023). Global Coaching Study 2023 Executive Summary. https://coachingfederation.org/app/uploads/2023/04/2023ICFGlobalCoachingStudy_ExecutiveSummary.pdf.

Institute of Coaching (n.d.) Anthony Grant PhD. https://instituteofcoaching.org/anthony-grant-phd. Retrieved 16 October 2024.

ISCP. (2023). About the International Society for Coaching Psychology. https://www.isfcp.info/.

Jones, R. J. (2021). *Coaching with Research in Mind.* Routledge.

Kimsey-House, H., Kimsey-House, K., Sandahl, P., Whitworth, L., & Phillips, A. (2018). *Co-active Coaching: The Proven Framework for Transformative Conversations at Work and in Life.* Hachette.

Linley, A. P.. & Harrington, S. (2008). Integrating positive psychology and coaching psychology: Shared assumptions and aspirations? In S. Palmer & A. Whybrow, (eds), *Handbook of Coaching Psychology* (pp. 40–56). Routledge.

Palmer, S., & Whybrow, A. (2005). The proposal to establish a special group in coaching psychology. *The Coaching Psychologist, 1*(1), 5–12.

Palmer, S., & Whybrow, A. (2008a). Coaching psychology: An introduction. In S. Palmer & A. Whybrow (eds), *Handbook of Coaching Psychology* (pp. 1–20). Routledge.

Palmer, S., & Whybrow, A. (eds). (2008b). *Handbook of Coaching Psychology.* Routledge.

Palmer, S., & Whybrow, A. (2017). *What do Coaching Psychologists and Coaches Really Do? Results from Two International Surveys.* Invited paper at the 7th International Congress of Coaching Psychology, London, 18 October.

Palmer, S., & Whybrow, A. (eds). (2019). *Handbook of Coaching Psychology* (2nd edition). Routledge.

Panchal, S., Palmer, S., & Green, S. (2019). From positive psychology to the development of positive psychology coaching. In S. Palmer & A. Whybrow (eds), *Handbook of Coaching Psychology* (pp. 51–67). Routledge.

Passmore, J., & Lai, Y. L. (2021). Coaching psychology: Exploring definitions and research contribution to practice. In J. Passmore & D. Tee (eds), *Coaching Researched: A Coaching Psychology Reader* (pp. 3–22). Wiley.

Performance Consultants (2024). Sir John Whitmore. https://www.performanceconsultants.com/about-us/sir-john-whitmore/.

Seligman, M. E. P. (2002). *Authentic Happiness: Using the New Positive Psychology to Realize your Potential for Lasting Fulfillment.* Free Press

Sherman, S., & Freas, A. (2004). The wild west of executive coaching. *Harvard Business Review, 82*(11), 82–93.

Smith, W. A., Boniwell, I., & Green, S. (2021). *Positive Psychology Coaching in the Workplace.* Springer.

Sorensen, S. (2022). Celebrating coaching's fire starter, Professor Anthony Grant. https://www.aretecoach.io/post/taking-out-the-sham-putting-in-the-wham-celebrating-coaching-s-fire-starter-dr-anthony-grant.

Whitmore, J. (1992). *Coaching for Performance: A Practical Guide to Growing Your Own Skills.* Nicholas Brealey Publishing.

Whitmore, J. (2002). *Coaching for Performance: GROWing People, Performance and Purpose.* NB Publishing.

Whybrow, A., & Palmer, S. (2019). Past, present and future. In S. Palmer, S. & A. Whybrow (eds), *Handbook of Coaching Psychology* (2nd edition, pp. 5–13). Routledge.

Section 2

Key Theories

This section in summary:

- Person-centred theory has developed from the work of psychologist Carl Rogers, who proposed that people have an innate drive to grow, that the environment can facilitate or hinder this, each person is their own best expert in how to develop, and the job of a therapist is to provide the right conditions for growth rather than to direct growth.
- The human tendency towards self-actualisation, reaching one's own potential in line with one's innate needs, is a fundamental assumption in person-centred theory.
- Self-actualising can be negative though, if the person actualises in line with external influences rather than their own innate needs.
- Unconditional positive regard, where a person is accepted for who they are and no conditions are placed upon them, is a key environmental influence to help people achieve positive self-actualisation.
- Person-centred theories share assumptions with some more contemporary psychological theories, particularly self-determination theory from within the positive psychology tradition.
- Person-centred theory is seen as a foundational concept in coaching psychology, directing attention towards the importance of creating an authentic, trusting, and

DOI: 10.4324/9781032686448-4

empathic relationship where unconditional positive regard can be demonstrated. It also steers the coach towards being non-directive in their approach, allowing the coachee to direct the coaching.

- In practice, person-centred theories emphasise the importance of key coaching competencies, including active listening, questioning skills, and reflecting. The coach takes the mindset that the coachee is whole, resourceful, and able to develop.
- Goals are standards by which individuals can judge their performance.
- There is a wealth of evidence in psychology to suggest that setting specific and challenging goals can improve performance when we know the behaviours needed to achieve the goal and feel competent to perform these.
- These types of goals help us to direct our attention to goal-relevant activities, persist over time and in the face of obstacles, and gather goal-relevant knowledge.
- Most coaching involves some degree of goal-setting, although the evidence on the impact of goal-setting in coaching is more sparse than in other areas.
- Coaches can use the contracting processes to help define goals that are meaningful to the coachee, but these must be open to change as the coachee discovers new things about themselves through the coaching engagement.
- Learning involves changing how we respond to a stimulus as a result of some aspect of our experience.
- Adult learning is distinguished from that of children, as adults have a wealth of experience to draw upon.
- Knowles' theory of andragogy proposes that adults learn when they perceive a need to, they draw on their experiences, they are self-directed in their learning, and they can apply the results of their learning to their current situation.

- Mezirow's theory of transformational learning proposes that learning occurs when current frames of reference are disrupted, which provides an opening for learning and change.
- Both andragogy and transformational learning place reflection as a central element in adult learning. Kolb's experiential learning cycle provides a model of how experience is transformed into learning via reflection.
- Providing time and space for reflection is a key part of facilitating growth in coachees and in coach development.
- Coaches can follow the principles of adult learning theories by ensuring that they allow the coachee to set their own goals, provide an unhurried environment to allow time for reflection, and support the coachee's reflective skills using questioning skills and tools and techniques from various coaching approaches.
- Coaching psychologists can draw from a variety of psychological theories, each with different assumptions about the nature of human development.
- Behavioural theories assume that people learn via experiences that shape behaviour. Behaviourist coaching approaches often emphasise goals and focus on the behaviours that will enable goal achievement.
- Cognitive behavioural theories suggest that how we think about events mediates the relationship between events and our emotional and behavioural responses to them. The focus of cognitive behavioural coaching is to help the coachee explore their thoughts and beliefs as well as the impact these have, updating any unhelpful thoughts.
- Psychodynamic theory emphasises the importance of the unconscious in driving human behaviour. Psychodynamic coaches will pay particular attention to what the coachee may *not* be aware of and provide a safe space to allow this material to surface, leading to insights for the coachee.

- Systems theory shifts focus away from the individual to the wider systems they are, and have been, a part of. A systemic coach will ask a coachee to consider the wider system they are operating in, helping the coachee to gain insights into the forces operating in this system.
- Psychological approaches to coaching differ in the extent to which they focus on the individual or wider organisational factors and on improving performance or developing insights.
- While some coaches operate as purists within one tradition or another, most will take a more eclectic approach, using elements of different psychological theories to suit the presenting needs of the coachee.

Chapter 3

Person-Centred Theories

What is it?

Person-centred coaching psychology takes its assumptions from person-centred therapy, which developed in the 1950s, mainly from the work of the psychologist Carl Rogers (Rogers, 1951, 1957, 1959, 1961). Rogers' work signified a shift away from the medical model in psychology, where people were assumed to be damaged or needed "fixing".

> **Person-centred coaching psychology.** A coaching approach with roots in the humanistic tradition, which emphasises a supportive, non-directive relationship between coach and coachee.

Instead, Rogers' person-centred approach made four key assertions:

- People have the capacity to grow and develop to reach their highest potential.
- Growth does not happen automatically and requires certain social conditions to occur.
- Each person is their own best expert in what they need to grow and develop.
- The job of a therapist, counsellor, or coach is not to judge or direct the coachee, but simply to provide the right social conditions for growth to occur.

DOI: 10.4324/9781032686448-5

There are many similarities between person-centred approaches and more contemporary approaches in psychology. Positive psychology coaching and humanistic coaching share very similar basic assumptions, including the natural human tendency towards growth and the need for favourable social conditions to support this growth (Gregory & Levy, 2013), although the level of focus may differ (Patterson & Joseph, 2007). This chapter will therefore draw on evidence taken from these approaches, as well as specifically looking at person-centred coaching.

What is the underpinning psychology?

The fullest account of Rogers' original theory is given in his 1959 chapter "A theory of therapy, personality and interpersonal relationships as developed in the client-centred framework". Two propositions that are key to coaching based on the extensive work of Rogers and his colleagues are the self-actualising tendency and unconditional positive regard.

Self-actualising tendency. The assumption that humans have an innate capacity for, and motivation towards, growth and development in ways that serve that individual. **Unconditional positive regard.** Where conditions are not imposed on the worth of an individual.

Self-actualising tendency

The first assumption of person-centred approaches is that humans have an innate capacity for, and motivation towards, growth and development in ways that serve that individual. This includes not only what is needed to preserve life, but also what is needed to achieve pleasure, creativity, and to learn and develop. The last of these is often referred to as self-actualising. While many readings of person-centred theory assume that self-actualising is always positive, this tendency towards growth may actually be dysfunctional depending upon the environmental conditions. This is at odds with the way the term growth is commonly used today, which also assumes growth is positive.

Functional growth and **dysfunctional growth** are distinguished in person-centred theory by the extent to which the growth is aligned with the individual's **innate needs**. Under favourable social conditions, experiences are interpreted and growth can occur in line with innate needs. Examples are following your interests to study history at university; leaving a romantic relationship that no longer makes you happy; requesting a job share to take up duties that you feel will be more fulfilling. Under less favourable social conditions, experiences may not be accurately perceived (or not perceived at all), or they may be evaluated in reference to external values (e.g., the views of others), rather than what we innately need. Examples are taking over the family business because it is expected of you; developing a specific look because it is admired by your peer group; not questioning an unethical decision at work because you do not want to cause a confrontation. In both functional and dysfunctional growth, the person changes and grows, but only functional growth is likely to result in positive outcomes for the individual. Dysfunctional growth can lead to tension and dissatisfaction for the individual, as what they are working towards does not actually meet their innate needs.

> **Functional growth.** When psychological growth occurs in line with innate needs.
>
> **Dysfunctional growth.** When psychological growth occurs in line with external factors rather than innate needs.
>
> **Innate needs.** Fundamental, inborn requirements that are essential for human growth and wellbeing.

Conditions in the environment can impact whether a person experiences functional or dysfunctional growth. Rogers identified that one key way a therapist can facilitate functional growth is through providing unconditional positive regard.

Unconditional positive regard

The most significant environmental factor in supporting functional growth is the unconditional positive regard of significant others. This means that conditions are not imposed on the worth of the individual. For example, parents still show love, warmth, and affection for their children even if they have not tidied their bedrooms. Romantic partners continue to be supportive and caring when we have had a bad day and are moody. Friends stick by us when we are having a difficult time and we do not call as much as we used to. Under these conditions, the individual is free to develop in ways that align with their innate needs and therefore they can experience functional growth.

However, if significant others impose what are known as **conditions of worth** (i.e., their positive regard, love, esteem etc. is contingent on the individual acting in a certain way), these

> **Conditions of worth.** Where external evaluations of what is judged as "good" are imposed on another.

external evaluations of what is "good" can be internalised by the individual and can then serve to guide self-actualisation towards these externally imposed values, rather than those that are intrinsically valued by the individual. This is when dysfunctional growth can occur.

Person-centred theory and contemporary psychological theories

Person-centred theory shares some fundamental, **meta-theoretical** assumptions with more contemporary psychological theories, including

> **Meta-theoretical.** A focus on the underlying assumptions, frameworks, and methodologies that shape the development of theories.

self-determination theory (Deci & Ryan, 1985) from the positive psychology tradition (see Chapter 2 for a discussion of positive psychology).

Like person-centred theory, self-determination theory takes the view that

> **Self-determination theory.** A theory that emphasises the importance of autonomy, competence, and relatedness as needs that must be met for optimal wellbeing and growth.

humans are inherently predisposed towards growth, maximising their potential within the environment in which they operate. Being from the positive psychology tradition, self-determination theory also shares with person-centred theory an emphasis on positivity and the coachee's wellbeing (Gregory & Levy, 2013).

Both person-centred theory and self-determination theory propose that the environment can help or hinder functional growth, and certain conditions need to be present within the environment to allow self-actualisation (Patterson & Joseph, 2007). While Rogers emphasised the importance of unconditional positive regard in the environment for positive growth to occur, self-determination theory identifies three elements that need to be present:

- **competence**
- **autonomy**
- **relatedness**.

Research and theorising in positive psychology, and self-determination theory in particular, can support the evidence base for person-centred approaches, which is lacking compared to the evidence bases for

> **Competence.** This is the need to feel good at things and to feel able to cope in our environment.
> **Autonomy.** The need to have control over our own attitudes and behaviour.
> **Relatedness.** The need to be in relationships with others; to care for and be cared for by others.

approaches such as cognitive-behavioural therapy (Patterson & Joseph, 2007).

Why is it important to coaches?

Many of the assumptions of coaching are shared by person-centred theory. Indeed, coaching can be seen as having roots in person-centred approaches. The definitions of coaching given in Chapter 1 include ideas such as outcomes being of value to the coachee, that coaching is about maximising potential, and that the aim of coaching is to facilitate the growth of individuals and teams. Both person-centred theory and coaching theory assume that the coachee is best placed to decide on what they need and how to achieve this and the work of the coach is not to provide direction, but instead to provide the conditions under which the coachee can identify their own path.

Despite the proliferation of theories, models, and tools that have been applied to coaching, many of which will be covered in the following chapters, the principles of person-centred theory guide what can be seen as the most fundamental element of coaching: the relationship.

Box 3.1   The importance of the relationship in coaching

Many research studies have sought to establish what are the most important "ingredients" in effective coaching. For example: Does it matter what tools and techniques the coach uses? Does meeting face-to-face rather than online make a difference? Are external coaches better than internal coaches? The one thing that consistently emerges as being significantly linked to coaching outcomes is the quality of the relationship between the coach and the coachee. De Haan and Gannon (2017) summarise 16 studies that examine the importance of the relationship in coaching. The vast majority of these studies support the importance of the relationship in effective coaching engagements and particular elements of the person-centred approach consistently emerge as being critical. The results show that in high-quality coaching relationships there must be trust, coaches must show **empathy** and unconditional positive regard for the coachee, and they

---

must be genuine and authentic. These mirror the conditions Rogers originally outlined for effective, person-centred therapeutic relationships.

Empathy. The ability to understand and share another person's feelings or experiences.

However, Grant (2014) identified that goal-focused coaching relationships have a clearer impact on outcomes than humanistic, person-centred relationships, therefore the quality of the relationship may not be the only factor influencing the effectiveness of coaching.

The working alliance

A term that is closely associated with the quality of the relationship in coaching and other helping professions is the **working alliance.** The working alliance has its history in psychotherapy (Horvath et al., 2011) but has since been applied to coaching (e.g., O'Broin & Palmer, 2009). Features of a strong working alli-

Working alliance. A collaborative relationship between a coach and coachee that is argued to be influential in achieving desired outcomes.

ance include coach and coachee agreement on goals and on the tasks that need to be accomplished, a bond that includes trust, respect, and care for one another, a commitment to responsibilities in the relationship, and active engagement in the relationship (see Graßmann et al., 2020).

In line with person-centred theory, scholars who advocate for the importance of the working alliance believe that the quality of this relationship is crucial in achieving positive outcomes in helping professions. The elements identified as necessary in the bond between coach and coachee align with Rogers' proposed ingredients of a strong relationship in person-centred approaches. Trust can be defined as

> the willingness of a party to be vulnerable to the actions of another party based on the expectation that the other will perform a particular action important to the trustor, irrespective of the ability to monitor or control that other party.
>
> (Mayer et al., 1995)

Where a coach displays unconditional positive regard, the coachee can trust that whatever they say the coach will still demonstrate respect for them. Likewise, if the coach presents as authentic in the relationship, then the coachee can trust that what the coach is saying to them is true. Care refers to the coach's genuine concern for the wellbeing and development of the coachee. Unconditional positive regard demonstrates care for the coachee, as the coach makes the coachee feel accepted and cared for regardless of their thoughts, feelings, or behaviours. Empathy also links to care, as an empathic coach demonstrates that they understand and care about the feelings of the coachee.

In their **meta-analysis**, Graßmann and colleagues (2020) found that the quality of the working alliance between coach and coachee was positively associated with desired outcomes from coaching (such as sat-

> **Meta-analysis.** A statistical technique used to combine results from multiple studies addressing the same or similar research questions.

isfaction, self-awareness, and goal attainment), negatively associated with undesired outcomes from coaching (such as reduced job satisfaction), and was robust across type of coachees, coaches' expertise, number of coaching sessions, and coachees' or coaches' perspectives. Research such as this supports the importance of the relationship in coaching, indirectly supporting the propositions of person-centred coaching.

With person-centred relationship principles being so key to outcomes in coaching, the next section describes in more detail how a coach could achieve these in practice. It should be stated, however, that taking a person-centred approach does not preclude the use of other tools and techniques, many of which are founded upon very different theoretical approaches to change. A person-centred approach can be the basis for an effective coaching relationship, onto which other approaches can be added (Gregory & Levy, 2013).

How is it applied in practice?

Person-centred coaching is not comprised of a set of tools and techniques for a coach to use, rather it is about the **mindset** a coach takes to the coaching engagement. The person-centred coach believes that the coachee has the innate ability and motivation to grow and is also the expert in how they

> **Mindset.** The mental framework that shapes how an individual thinks, feels, and behaves.

achieve that (Joseph & Bryant-Jefferies, 2019). This concept of mindset has strong connections to coaching professional body competencies. For example, the ICF has a competency entitled "Embodies a coaching mindset", which includes believing that coachees are whole or complete, resourceful, and in charge of their own outcomes (ICF, 2024).

The role of the coach is, therefore, to create the right conditions and relationship to facilitate this growth. This also links to the importance of the relationship in coaching, as discussed earlier, where the coach needs to develop a relationship with the coachee that demonstrates that they hold these core beliefs about the coachee.

Gregory and Levy (2013) outline some ways in which a person-centred coach will work. One of these is that the coach will enable the coachee to bring their full, authentic self to the coaching relationship. Demonstrating unconditional positive regard will be a key part of enabling this. The coach will also ensure that the coaching conversation focuses on the coachee in a holistic manner. For example, if the coachee is discussing an issue at work, the coach may enquire whether the same issue shows up in other areas of the coachee's life. Exploring both positive and negative aspects of the coachee's experience is also a way in which a person-centred coach will ensure they are serving the "whole" coachee.

A person-centred coach will also be focused on helping the coachee to achieve self-actualisation. A coachee may not know what self-actualisation is for them, so the coach can facilitate an exploration of this. One tool which originates from positive psychology coaching is the "ideal future self" task (Kauffman et al., 2009), where the coachee is asked to consider what their best self in their best possible future would look like, without any constraints. Exploring this desired future then helps to bring clarity regarding the coachee's innate needs, rather than what may be imposed upon them by external constraints. This can help to ensure that growth is functional, rather than dysfunctional. The coach can then support the coachee to set goals and create an action plan for how they might achieve this desired future.

Person-centred coaching encourages self-motivated action by the coachee and facilitation of that process by the coach. The coach should not be an "expert" or teacher in the coaching relationship. This means that the coach acts in a non-directive manner, taking their lead from the coachee and facilitating the coachee's learning and development in whatever way the coachee wants. Key skills in coaching, including **active listening**, asking open questions, and **reflecting back** a coachee's words, are essential in this non-directive approach. Again, this links closely to coaching professional body competencies. For example, the European Mentoring and Coaching Council (EMCC, 2015) include using an active listening style and a range of questioning techniques to raise awareness in their "Enabling insight and learning" competency category.

Active listening. Paying close attention to what is said, what is not said, and non-verbal communication. This requires the listener to be fully present and engaged in the conversation.

Reflecting back. The process of mirroring or paraphrasing the coachee's words.

Person-centred approaches are the bedrock of effective coaching for many, however there are authors in the field who assert that taking a purely person-centred approach to coaching may have some potential pitfalls, for example in neglecting the important role that challenge plays in effective coaching.

Box 3.2   The importance of challenge

Day (2021) contests the generally accepted, person-centred view of coaching as being the only way to coach. Although the origins of coaching reside in person-centred approaches, and the professional body competency frameworks generally highlight skills consistent with this approach, Day asserts that there are three key risks in adopting a purely person-centred approach:

- *Collusion.* The coach fails to ask questions that challenge assumptions or give feedback from an alternative perspective.
- *Irrelevance.* The coachee chooses to talk about things that are not relevant to their goal, rather than addressing key issues, and the coach follows their agenda.
- *Self-obsession.* Focusing solely on the coachee's agenda can mean that awareness of the wider context and connections are missed and the focus is very narrowly on the self.

Day argues that these risks mean that coachees may not make the greatest gains in awareness or the most substantial changes under a purely non-directive coaching approach. While the coach needs to be supportive, he argues that challenge is also needed to ensure that the coaching is truly powerful.

Coaches may provide challenge in a number of ways. For example, to avoid collusion a coach may provide feedback to the coachee on their own feelings or offer an alternative interpretation of a situation. To combat irrelevance, the coach can ask questions that tap into why the current topic is important to the coachee and how it relates to their goals.

The perspectives of wider stakeholders, such as the organisation or colleagues, can be brought in via questions that ask the coachee to consider how these stakeholders would view the situation. Techniques such as constellations (see Chapter 6), which enable mapping of the wider system, could also be useful to challenge a self-focused coachee to consider wider implications.

Further reading and resources

Day, I. (2024, July). Coaching is simple, isn't it? – Carl Rogers core conditions [Post]. LinkedIn. https://www.linkedin.com/posts/iand ay_coaching-part-time-courses-activity-7212382272669265921-pAOE?utm_source=share&utm_medium=member_desktop.

Joseph, S. (2006). *Person-Centred Coaching Psychology: A Meta-Theoretical Perspective*. British Psychological Society.

PsychotherapyNet (2012, November 14). *Carl Rogers on Person-Centered Therapy* [Video]. YouTube. https://youtu.be/o0neRQzudzw?si=w4EpqcN_6fO6pr4I.

References

Day, I. (2021). Balancing challenge and support in coaching. In J. Passmore (ed.), *The Coaches' Handbook: The Complete Practitioner Guide for Professional Coaches*. Routledge.

Deci, E. L., & Ryan, R. M. (1985). *Intrinsic Motivation and Self-Determination in Human Behavior*. Plenum.

De Haan, E., & Gannon, J. (2017). The coaching relationship. In T. Bachkirova, G. Spence, & D. Drake (eds), *The SAGE Handbook of Coaching* (pp. 195–217). Sage.

EMCC (2015). *EMCC Global Professional Practice Framework for Mentors, Coaches and Leaders Specific to Role and Context*. https://emccdrive.emccglobal.org/api/file/download/5uLuRItx5eyXPtvpjH4u5hm32IQQOtng8AY9m6JA.

Grant, A. M. (2014). Autonomy support, relationship satisfaction and goal focus in the coach–coachee relationship: Which best predicts coaching success? *Coaching: An International Journal of Theory, Research and Practice, 7*(1), 18–38.

Graßmann, C., Schölmerich, F., & Schermuly, C. C. (2020). The relationship between working alliance and coachee outcomes in coaching:

A meta-analysis. *Human Relations*, *73*(1), 35–58. https://doi.org/10.1177/0018726718819725.

Gregory, J. B., & Levy, P. P. (2013). Humanistic/person-centred approaches. In J. Passmore, D. B. Peterson, & T. Freire (eds), *The Wiley-Blackwell Handbook of The Psychology of Coaching and Mentoring* (pp. 285–297). Wiley-Blackwell.

Horvath, A. O., Del Re, A. C., Flückiger, C., & Symonds, D. (2011). Alliance in individual psychotherapy. *Psychotherapy*, *48*(1), 9.

ICF (2024). ICF core competencies. https://coachingfederation.org/credentials-and-standards/core-competencies.

Joseph, S., & Bryant-Jefferies, R. (2019). Person-centred coaching psychology. In S. Palmer & A. Whybrow (eds), *Handbook of Coaching Psychology: A Guide for Practitioners*. Routledge.

Kauffman, C., Boniwell, I., & Silberman, J. (2009). The positive psychology approach to coaching. In E. Cox, T. Bachkirova, & D. Clutterbuck (eds), *The Complete Handbook of Coaching* (pp. 158–171). Sage.

Mayer, R. C., Davis, J. H., & Schoorman, F. D. (1995). An integrative model of organizational trust. *The Academy of Management Review*, *20*(3), 709–734. https://doi.org/10.2307/258792.

O'Broin, A., & Palmer, S. (2009). Co-creating an optimal coaching alliance: A cognitive behavioural coaching perspective. *International Coaching Psychology Review*, *4*(2), 184–194.

Patterson, T. G., & Joseph, S. (2007). Person-centered personality theory: Support from self-determination theory and positive psychology. *Journal of Humanistic Psychology*, *47*(1), 117–139.

Rogers, C. (1951) *Client-Centered Therapy*. Houghton Mifflin.

Rogers, C. R. (1957). The necessary and sufficient conditions of therapeutic personality change. *Journal of Consulting Psychology*, *21*, 95–103.

Rogers, C. R. (1959). A theory of therapy, personality and interpersonal relationships as developed in the client-centred framework. In S. Koch (ed.), *Psychology: A Study of a Science*, Vol. 3: *Formulations of the Person and the Social Context* (pp. 184–256). McGraw-Hill.

Rogers, C. R. (1961). *On Becoming a Person*. Houghton Mifflin.

Chapter 4

Goal-Setting Theory

What is it?

The importance of goals and **goal-setting** has been researched in psychology long before coaching psychology came about. Grant and O'Connor (2022) discuss various definitions of goals, highlighting that many include cognitive (what we think we want to achieve), affective (how we feel about the goal), and behavioural (what we might do to achieve our goal) elements. They highlight however that many of these definitions are unwieldy and therefore not helpful. A more recent, succinct definition is provided by Jones where goals are defined as "an explicit standard by which individuals can judge their progress and performance" (Jones, 2021, p. 99).

> **Goal-setting.** The process of identifying and clarifying what you want to accomplish.

Setting goals is thought to be a crucial part of **self-regulation** (Grant, 2012) and enhances performance (Jones, 2021). This has been researched in a variety of domains, including in education and in the workplace. Those who set themselves specific and challenging goals achieve more than those who do not engage in goal-setting.

> **Self-regulation.** The ability to manage and control one's emotions, thoughts, and behaviours.

DOI: 10.4324/9781032686448-6

What is the underpinning theory?

The authors that are most widely cited in relation to theory and research on goal-setting are Locke and Latham (1990). They proposed that goals increase performance when the goal meets the following criteria:

- The goal is clear and specific.
- The goal is sufficiently challenging and compelling.
- The individual understands what behaviours will lead to goal-achievement.
- The individual feels competent to execute those behaviours.

In addition to the above criteria, **feedback** is also powerful in ensuring that goals increase performance, with self-generated feedback having the greatest impact. The

Feedback. Providing information about someone's performance or behaviour.

need for goals to be broken down into manageable sub-goals has also been highlighted (Eldridge & Dembkowski, 2013).

As well as establishing the conditions under which goals improve performance, Locke and Latham (2006) also proposed the mechanisms by which goals impact upon performance. The first mechanism they suggest is that goals work by directing our attention and effort. At any given moment, there are thousands of demands competing for our attention. Having specific goals can help us to keep our attention focused on task-relevant information and activities, and also help us to use **conscious** attention switching processes to focus on what matters to us in the moment. Without having a conscious goal in mind, whatever is most attention grabbing will be what we focus on, regardless of whether it moves us towards our aims or not.

Conscious. Something that an individual is aware of.

The second way Locke and Latham (2006) propose that goals influence performance is through increasing enthusiasm and persistence. Pritchard and colleagues (2008) relate this to humans having an "energy pool". Different people will have different "pool" sizes and within people the size of "pool" will vary across time. Regardless of the size of the "pool", simply having one implies that there is a limited amount of energy that we can expend, and we have to decide how to allocate that energy. Having a goal makes us feel more enthusiastic in relation to expending energy on the behaviours needed to achieve that goal, which in turn leads to allocating more energy to task-relevant behaviours.

Having a goal also increases persistence in goal-relevant behaviours. Negative emotions related to setbacks have less impact on us if we have a clear goal, and we are more likely to continue to invest energy in the face of adversity. There is a caveat here though: while challenging goals have been found to be more motivating and lead to increased performance (Locke & Latham, 1990), the goal cannot be so challenging that we experience consistent sub-goal failure (Jones, 2021). Box 4.1 discusses the implications of goal failure.

For goals to increase our enthusiasm and persistence, they must be important and meaningful to us (Jones, 2021). Goals that do not align with our **values** are unlikely to lead to increased enthusiasm, persistence, and hence performance, because achieving them does not bring us closer to what we really want in life.

> **Values**. Deeply held beliefs or principles that influence decisions and behaviour.

The final mechanism proposed is an increase in task-relevant knowledge that follows from setting a goal, which then increases performance (Jones, 2021). When we set a goal, we scan our **subconscious** for relevant knowledge that we can bring to bear on achievement of that goal. If the goal involves tasks that are new to us, then the

> **Subconscious**. Something that an individual is not fully aware of, but can access with focused effort.

goal promotes planning of how we can acquire the knowledge that we need to be successful. This increase in knowledge then helps to boost our performance.

Box 4.1 Goal failure

Jones (2021) discusses that whilst challenging goals are likely to be motivating, if we set our sights too high and therefore experience frequent sub-goal failures as a consequence, this can reduce our motivation and persistence in achieving our goals. For example, if I wish to read ten academic articles a day, but I also have to deliver two classes each day, and see my personal tutees, and write new course material and respond to emails, it is unlikely that I will be able to achieve my goal. While this problem may be alleviated by making the goal less challenging (e.g., read one academic paper a day), a less challenging goal may not align with my values (being a knowledgeable academic) or my dream goal (becoming a professor), so it may lose its motivational power another way.

Jones (2021) outlines several strategies that can help to alleviate the negative impact of sub-goal failure on goal attainment. These including making changes to the situations that we place ourselves in and changing the way we appraise situations cognitively, either before we enter them or after we have experienced them. For example, I might choose not to have lunch in the cafeteria where I know I will end up getting asked lots of questions by colleagues and students and instead use this time to read a paper. If I fail to read the ten papers I set out to, I may decide not to focus on how I missed the goal, but on what enabled me to successfully read the six papers I did.

A specific strategy that can be used is having "emergency reserves" (Sharif & Shu, 2017), whereby I set my sub-goal (read ten papers a day), but I have a number of "emergency reserves" that I can deploy on days when I know I won't be able to meet this target (i.e., I have a number of days when I know I'm allowed to read fewer than ten papers). In their research, Sharif and Shu (2017) found that people who set goals that included emergency reserves were more likely to persist after a sub-goal failure.

Managing goal failure is an important consideration, as goal failure can lead to acute and chronic distress (Jones et al., 2013), which is ultimately unhelpful in the context of longer-term persistence towards goals.

Within the psychological literature on goal-setting, there has been an attempt to distinguish between different types of goals and the impact they can have on performance. Grant and O'Connor (2022) outline a number of ways in which goals can be distinguished from one another, including timeframe and goal orientation.

Timeframe

Goals can be long-term visions of what we want our life to be like in the future (e.g., an undergraduate student envisioning themself as having a successful career in marketing, owning their own house and car). Alternatively, goals can be shorter term (e.g., the same undergraduate student wanting to finish writing an assignment by the end of the weekend). Grant and O'Connor (2022) identify these as being **distal goals** and **proximal goals** respectively. This distinction aligns with Whitmore's (2017) goal-setting pyramid in coaching. He places **dream goals**, which are akin to the distal, long-term goals, at the top of the hierarchy. Then there are the **end goals**: these are what we must achieve to make the dream goal a reality. In our student example, this might be securing a job in a marketing agency that pays at least £30,000 a year. The next level is **performance goals**: these identify the specific and tangible standards we

Distal goals. Longer-term goals.
Proximal goals. Shorter-term goals.
Dream goals. Longer-term, life ambitions.
End goals. What must be achieved to make the dream goal a reality.

must meet to achieve the end goal. For example, our student might need to graduate with at least a 2:1 from their programme and get marketing experience before they graduate. Finally, we have **process goals**. These are the steps that are needed to achieve all the levels of goals

Performance goals. Specific and tangible standards an individual must meet to achieve their end goals.

Process goals. Short-term goals that specify what an individual aims to achieve "right now" in service of their performance goals.

described above. Process goals are like proximal goals, in that they specify what we are aiming to achieve right now. To be motivating, the goals at all levels need to be aligned, they need to be meaningful, and they need to be sufficiently specific and challenging.

Grant and O'Connor (2022) place further importance on understanding the hierarchy of goals by highlighting that when we fail to focus sufficiently on distal goals, our behaviour becomes guided by proximal goals. Proximal goals are not usually motivating in and of themselves, and so can lead to goal dissatisfaction and goal disengagement if the broader value is forgotten.

Goal orientation

Dweck (2006) outlined a theory of **goal orientation** that distinguishes between **mastery-oriented goals** (or learning-oriented) and **performance-oriented goals**. Individuals with a mastery orientation generally believe that their skills and abilities are

Goal orientation. The underlying attitude individuals hold towards the goals they set.

Mastery-oriented goals. Goals that focus on learning and development.

Performance-oriented goals. Goals that focus on demonstrating achievement.

malleable, and that they can develop and improve if they put in sufficient time and effort. This is sometimes referred to as having a growth mindset. In contrast, those with a performance orientation believe that abilities are generally fixed, and they are more concerned with demonstrating their competence rather than learning new things. This can be called a fixed mindset.

Another way in which goal orientation has been distinguished is between **approach goals** and **avoidance goals**. Approach goals are framed in terms of achieving something desirable, whereas avoidance goals are framed as avoiding something that is unwanted (Grant & O'Connor, 2022). Table 4.1 gives some example goals with different combinations of orientations.

Approach goals. Goals that are framed in terms of achieving something desirable.
Avoidance goals. Goals that are framed in terms of avoiding something undesirable.

People will have a natural preference in their goal orientation, and this can have an impact on both performance and wellbeing. Research has shown that those with a mastery orientation generally set themselves more challenging goals, allocate more effort to achieving challenging goals, and are more likely to persist in the face of difficulties than those with performance goals (Jones,

Table 4.1 Example approach and avoidance and mastery and performance goals in the context of learning Spanish

	Mastery-oriented	Performance-oriented
Approach	I want to learn Spanish, increasing my current vocabulary and improving my knowledge of grammar and syntax.	I want to be able to have a conversation in Spain with a native Spanish speaker.
Avoid	I don't want to forget the Spanish that I have already learned.	I don't want to be embarrassed by not understanding a Spanish conversation.

2021). Grant and O'Connor (2022) summarise research that suggests that those who set avoidance goals experience lower wellbeing.

Why is it important to coaching?

Goal-setting is seen by many coaching scholars as integral to coaching (e.g., Grant, 2014; Jones, 2021), with Grant arguing that "*Most coaching is inherently specifically outcome or goal focused*" (2014, p. 23). Many definitions of coaching include some element of goal-setting or goal-achievement. For example, as outlined in in Chapter 1, Bono and colleagues (2009) state that coaching is a one-to-one learning and development intervention that uses a collaborative, reflective, goal-focused relationship to achieve professional outcomes that are valued by the coachee.

While the above suggests that goal-setting is an accepted part of coaching, Grant and O'Connor (2022) suggest that this is not necessarily the case. They state that some argue that setting goals within coaching restricts the conversation, limits flexibility, creates a focus on measurable targets that may not be meaningful, and can lead to coaches encouraging coachees to work on goals regardless of whether or not they are suitable. Furthermore, some coaches claim to not use any form of goal-setting in their approach. Jones (2021) highlights that more experienced coaches often distance themselves from goal-setting in coaching. However, Eldridge and Dembkowski (2013) argue that it is goals that ensure coaching is a learning and development intervention and not just a conversation. The balance of evidence therefore suggests that goal-setting is important to most coaching interventions.

Reflecting the importance of goal-setting in coaching, goal-setting is part of most of the major psychological approaches to coaching. For example, it is a key part of **behavioural approaches** to coaching, where most novice

Behavioural approaches. A psychological approach that emphasises the role of the environment on influencing behaviour, including the role of reward and punishment.

coaches begin their learning. One of the most frequently used models within the behavioural approach is the GROW model (Whitmore, 2017). The "G" in the model stands for goals. Within the model, coaches are expected to explore what the coachee's goal is before they go on to consider the current situation and how the coachee moves on from that (see Chapter 6 for more details). Goal-setting is also part of cognitive behavioural coaching (Palmer & Szymanska, 2019; see Chapter 6 for more details). **Solution-focused coaching** often asks people to imagine they wake up one day and their goal is achieved, relating to more distal, dream goals (Middendorf, 2022). One approach to coaching where goal-setting is less prominent is **Gestalt coaching**, which instead focuses on working to raise awareness of the here and now in the coaching relationship to enable awareness and change (Spoth et al., 2013).

Solution-focused coaching. A coaching approach that emphasises the desired result and how to achieve it.

Gestalt coaching. A coaching approach that emphasises working with the whole person in the current moment, to raise awareness.

While we can therefore acknowledge that there is some disagreement on whether goal-setting is essential to coaching, most definitions and approaches include some element of goal-setting and it is therefore crucial that the coach is able to facilitate this. The ICF **core competencies** specify that coaches must be able to partner with coachees to establish overall goals for a coaching engagement and specific goals for the coaching session

Core competencies. Skills, knowledge, abilities, and attributes that are fundamental to success.

(ICF, 2024). Grant and O'Connor (2022) suggest that coaches who have only a superficial knowledge of goal-setting may not be able to support their coachees in setting goals that are meaningful, motivating, and help the coachee to move forward. Coaches must therefore have a deeper understanding of goal-setting to be effective practitioners.

Despite there being a wealth of generic literature to support the importance of goal-setting in contexts such as education and healthcare, there is relatively little research directly related to goal-setting in coaching. Müller and Kotte (2020) conducted a systematic literature review on the occurrence of goal activities in coaching and their association with outcomes. They synthesised findings of 24 empirical studies and found that previously researched goal activities encompass goal-setting, setting action/development plans and a goal-focused coach–coachee relationship. Coaches report that they work with goals frequently, while coachees report this to occur less. They found a mixed picture in relation to outcomes, with several studies suggesting a positive relationship between goal activities and coaching outcomes, whilst other studies reported no significant association. This lack of association seems to relate to both study design and chosen outcome measures. Their initial findings point to possible moderating variables (e.g., coachee characteristics, initiator of goal activity) and the potential challenges of involving organisational stakeholders in goal activities. They conclude that the scarcity of empirical research stands in contrast to the prominent role of goals in the coaching literature.

How is it applied in practice?

Goal-setting in most coaching engagements usually begins with **contracting**. While contracting involves much more than just setting goals, Foy (2021) suggests that

> **Contracting.** A coaching process where the desired outcomes and ways of working are agreed.

contracting for results (i.e., goals), is a key part of the contracting process. Contracting can occur at various levels – for example, if an organisation is paying for its employees to receive coaching then there will be a contract with the organisation, which will need to include some overall goals or objectives for the coaching programme. There will also be contracting at the individual (or team or group) level for the coaching intervention, which will include the goals for the overall coaching intervention (i.e., what does the coachee (team or group) want to have achieved by the time they have finished the agreed-upon number of coaching sessions). In open-ended coaching programmes, the coach may want to set up goals for a certain number of sessions – for example, the coachee may want to feel confident enough to apply for a promotion after six sessions. It is also important to contract for each session. In this contracting the coachee sets a goal that they want to achieve in that particular session. There are several models to support contracting for a coaching session, one of the most popular being the STOKERS model (Foy, 2021 adapted from Pedrick, 2020).

- The first "S" in STOKERS refers to the subject. What would the coachee like to focus on in the session?
- "T" is timing. What would the coachee like to get out of the time available in the coaching session in relation to their chosen subject?
- "O" is for outcome. What would a successful outcome from the session look like?
- "K" is knowledge. How will the coachee know whether they have achieved that outcome or not?
- "E" is essence. Why this is important to the coachee right now?
- "R" is role. How can the coach best support the coachee in achieving the outcome?
- Finally, "S" is for start. Where would the coachee like to begin?

There is clearly some overlap between STOKERS and models of goal-setting from disciplines other than coaching, most notably SMART goals (Specific, Measurable, Achievable, Realistic, and Timebound). The elements of STOKERS that take it beyond models like SMART are the essence and role elements. Exploring the essence of the goal (*why* it is important to the coachee) links us back to the timeframe of goals and goal hierarchies (see above). It is important that the coachee has clarity regarding why they want to work on a certain goal and what it means to them in order for it to be motivating. By asking the essence question in STOKERS, the coach can explore with the coachee what the goal truly is about. Foy (2021) provides an example of a coachee wanting to become a millionaire. While that could be made into a perfectly acceptable SMART goal, without understanding what becoming a millionaire would give the coachee that they do not have now, we are unlikely to be able to unlock the real motivation to achieve the goal. In other words, being a millionaire is likely to be an end goal that helps the coachee achieve some dream goal (e.g., escaping a job or home life that they hate, being able to do philanthropic work, travelling around the world, etc.).

Defining the role that the coach will play also makes STOKERS distinct from other goal-setting approaches. A coach could play many roles in supporting a coachee to achieve the goals that they set for themselves. They may want a coach to be there to listen to them only, they may want a coach to challenge them, they may want a coach to reflect back patterns and connections that they observe in them, they may want a coach to be an accountability partner and so on. This reflects the element of partnership in coaching, and the belief that the coachee is best placed to know what they need from a coach. Unlike some other approaches to goal-setting, which are prescriptive in the steps needed to success-fully set motivating goals, a coach needs to be flexible in the way they work with a coachee.

The need for flexibility is likely to continue throughout the coaching engagement. Lee (2013) discusses how the "real" goal for coaching is unlikely to present itself at the outset of the relation-ship. Coaches need to explore initial, stated needs using processes such as STOKERS to ensure that a clear goal is "nailed down". This enables the coach to continually return to the goal and check in on progress with the coachee. However, Lee (2013) acknow-ledges that the coachee's goal(s) are likely to change as a result of the coaching process. In good coaching, the coachee is likely to be discovering things about themselves as they progress through the coaching engagement, which may modify, or entirely change, the goals that they want to achieve. The coach must therefore be prepared to explore changes in direction with the coachee and trust that the coachee will know when their focus should change. It is not the role of the coach to hold a coachee to their initially stated goal regardless of whether it now feels appropriate to that coachee or not. Coaches therefore need to be open, flexible, and avoid getting too invested in the coachee's goals.

Further reading and resources

Dweck, C. S. (2017). *Mindset: Changing the Way You think To Fulfil Your Potential* (Updated edition). Robinson.

Six Seconds, The Emotional Intelligence Network (2020, 23 December). *Goal Setting in Coaching: How to use CONTRACTING to boost Client Engagement* [Video]. YouTube. https://youtu.be/_wJED2UU mSA?si=z10zkx8sovmSpd0h.

Wheatley, J., & Hawkins, Z. (2022, 4 April). Goal-setting in coaching (No. 027) [Audio podcast episode]. *The Coaching Crowd®* Podcast with Jo Wheatley & Zoe Hawkins.

References

Bono, J. E., Purvanova, R. K., Towler, A. J., & Peterson, D. B. (2009). A survey of executive coaching practices. *Personnel Psychology, 62*(2), 361–404.

Dweck, C. S. (2006). *Mindset: The New Psychology of Success.* Random House.

Eldridge, F., & Dembkowski, S. (2013). Behavioural coaching. In J. Passmore, D. B. Peterson, & T. Freire (eds), *The Wiley-Blackwell Handbook of The Psychology of Coaching and Mentoring.* Wiley-Blackwell.

Foy, K. (2021). Contracting in coaching. In J. Passmore (ed.), *The Coaches' Handbook: The Complete Practitioner Guide for Professional Coaches.* Routledge.

Grant, A. M. (2012). An integrated model of goal-focused coaching: An evidence-based framework for teaching and practice. *International Coaching Psychology Review, 7*(2), 146–165.

Grant, A. M. (2014). Autonomy support, relationship satisfaction and goal focus in the coach–coachee relationship: Which best predicts coaching success? *Coaching: An International Journal of Theory, Research and Practice, 7*(1), 18–38.

Grant, A. M., & O'Connor, S. (2022). Goals in coaching practice. In S. Greif, H. Moller, W. Scholl, J. Passmore, & F. Muller (eds), *International Handbook of Evidence-Based Coaching: Theory, Research and Practice* (pp. 391–406). Springer.

ICF (2024). ICF core competencies. https://coachingfederation.org/credentials-and-standards/core-competencies.

Jones, R. J. (2021). *Coaching with Research in Mind.* Routledge.

Jones, N. P., Papadakis, A. A., Orr, C. A., & Strauman, T. J. (2013). Cognitive processes in response to goal failure: A study of ruminative thought and its affective consequences. *Journal of Social and Clinical Psychology, 32*(5), 482–503.

Lee, R. J. (2013). The role of contracting in coaching: Balancing individual client and organisational issues. In J. Passmore, D. B. Peterson, & T. Freire (eds), *The Wiley-Blackwell Handbook of The Psychology of Coaching and Mentoring.* Wiley-Blackwell.

Locke, E. A., & Latham, G. P. (1990). *A Theory of Goal Setting & Task Performance.* Prentice-Hall.

Locke, E. A., & Latham, G. P. (2006). New directions in goal-setting theory. *Current Directions in Psychological Science, 15*(5), 265–268.

Middendorf, J. (2022). *Solution-Focused Business Coaching: A Guide for Individual and Team Coaching.* Springer.

Müller, A. A., & Kotte, S. (2020). Of SMART, GROW and goals gone wild: A systematic literature review on the relevance of goal activities in workplace coaching. *International Coaching Psychology Review, 15*(2), 69–97.

Palmer, S., & Szymanska, K. (2019). Cognitive behavioural coaching: An integrative approach. In S. Palmer & A. Whybrow (eds), *Handbook of Coaching Psychology: A Guide for Practitioners* (pp. 108–130). Routledge.

Passmore, J., Peterson, D. B., & Freire, T. (eds). (2019). *The Wiley-Blackwell Handbook of The Psychology of Coaching and Mentoring.* Wiley-Blackwell.

Pedrick, C. (2020). *Simplifying Coaching: How to Have More Transformational Conversations by Doing Less.* McGraw-Hill Education.

Pritchard, R. D., Harrell, M. M., DiazGranados, D., & Guzman, M. J. (2008). The productivity measurement and enhancement system: A meta-analysis. *Journal of Applied Psychology, 93*(3), 540.

Sharif, Marissa A., and Suzanne B. Shu. (2017). The benefits of emergency reserves: Greater preference and persistence for goals that have slack with a cost. *Journal of Marketing Research, 54*(3): 495–509.

Spoth, J., Toman, S., Leichtman, R., & Allan, J. (2013). Gestalt approach. In J. Passmore, D. B. Peterson, & T. Freire (eds), *The Wiley-Blackwell Handbook of The Psychology of Coaching and Mentoring.* Wiley-Blackwell.

Whitmore, J. (2017). *Coaching for Performance: The Principles and Practice of Coaching and Leadership.* NB Publishing.

Chapter 5

Adult Learning Theory

What is it?

Defining **learning** is not straightforward. The *Oxford English Dictionary* (2024) defines learning as "the acquisition of knowledge or skills through study, experience, or being taught". While this definition makes intuitive sense, it assumes that there is

Learning. The process whereby an individual's understanding of how to respond to stimuli (e.g., an event) changes as a result of experiencing something in their environment (e.g., getting hurt), that they perceive via their five senses.

always an outcome of learning (in this example in knowledge or skills), but this is not always the case (i.e., we can learn something but forget it or never implement it). Terms such as experience are also, in general, imprecisely defined (Lachman, 1997). To address these concerns, Lachman (1997, p. 477) proposed a more nuanced, although not very user-friendly, definition: "Learning is the process by which a relatively stable modification in stimulus-response relations is developed as a consequence of functional environmental interaction via the senses."

Lachman's definition separates the process of learning from the outcomes of learning, directs attention to changes in the stimulus-response relationship, which is a key part of learning as typically defined by psychologists, and removes vague words such

DOI: 10.4324/9781032686448-7

as experience. In layman's terms, learning is a process whereby our understanding of how to respond to stimuli (e.g., an event) changes as a result of experiencing something in our environment (e.g., getting hurt) that we perceive via our five senses.

When we think about learning in coaching we are typically thinking about working with adults, therefore it is important to consider how adult learning is specifically defined. Adult learning, also known as **andragogy**, is distinct from pedagogy which is focused on learning in children and young adults. Andragogy makes the assumption that adults can learn and can be motivated to learn, and that there are certain conditions that facilitate their learning.

> **Andragogy.** The theory and practice of adult learning.

What is the underpinning psychology?

Three major theories in adult learning include: Knowles' theory of andragogy, Mezirow's transformative learning theory, and Kolb's reflective learning cycle.

Knowles' theory of andragogy

Knowles' (1980, 1989) theory of andragogy takes a **constructionist approach** to adult learning. It posits that adults draw upon their experience to create new learning based on their previous understanding. This theory is specific to adult learners, as children do not have the same pool of experience from which to draw, therefore their experience of learning is different.

> **Constructionist approach.** An approach to learning theory that proposes that individuals construct their own understanding and knowledge of the world through experience and reflection.

Knowles and colleagues (2020) suggested that there are six principles of andragogy:

1 Adults need to perceive that there is a need for them to learn.
2 With age individuals become increasingly self-directed, and therefore adults like to be responsible for their own decisions.
3 The wealth of experiences that adults have can help or hinder their learning.
4 Adults seek learning when it is relevant to solving a problem or making a change in their lives.
5 Adults generally want to be able to apply the results of their learning to their lives relatively quickly.
6 While adults can respond to external motivators, such as money, they are generally motivated internally, for example by wanting to develop competence in an area.

Knowles' theory of andragogy has been praised for directing educators towards how to engage adult learners and is considered one of the most learner-centred approaches to adult education. However, there are issues with the theory, which include the assumptions that adults have relevant experiences that they can draw upon and that they are intrinsically motivated to learn. There is also a lack of consideration of how organisational and societal pressures may influence the adult learner (McGrath, 2009), although recent updates to the text include diversity and inclusion in adult learning (Knowles et al., 2020). For example, a busy single parent with a full-time job who has been sent on a course about accounting by their boss, when they have never learned anything about accounting previously, may struggle to engage with the programme no matter how well Knowles' principles are adhered to.

Mezirow's transformative learning theory

Mezirow (1990, 1997, 2000) presents an alternative view of adult learning, focusing on learning that results in shifts in thinking, which he termed **transformative learning**. In this theory, the experiences that adults accrue throughout their lives create **frames** of reference, or meaning perspectives, which govern how they see the world. Frames of reference allow us to operate in many different environments without needing to stop and consciously think about things; we interpret the information

> **Transformative learning.** Learning that results in shifts in thinking.
> **Frames of reference.** Mental structures through which individuals understand and interpret the world around them.

that we receive according to the frame of reference and we reject anything that does not fit with it. For example, we may have started our working life in a highly competitive organisation and acquired a frame of reference that leads us to see work as being competitive. As such, we interpret new situations in the workplace as being competitive without stopping to think if that is actually the case. Transformative learning changes any relevant frames of reference.

Transformative learning only occurs when some form of disruptive event, life challenge, or, as Mezirow (1990) phrased it, **"disorienting dilemma"** occurs. These kinds of experiences challenge the frame of reference, frustrate goal achievement, and create an opening for learning and change. For example, if an individual is sacked from

> **Disorienting dilemma.** An experience that challenges an individual's frame of reference, frustrates goal achievement, and creates an opening for learning and change.

a job role because they are too competitive and cause conflict with their colleagues, this may lead them to re-evaluate whether seeing the workplace as a competitive arena is actually serving them. Without such an event, it is unlikely that adults will be open to learning, as there is no need to critically examine their own frames of reference.

Once an opening to learning has occurred, then the following phases of transformation may be followed:

1 Self-examination of feelings that arise in relation to the disruption.
2 Critical assessment of assumptions that underpin the disruption and the resulting emotions, which can lead to significant insights.
3 Realisation that other people have experienced similar things and have managed to resolve the issue.
4 Exploration of different alternative frames of reference to replace the old one.
5 Planning actions that allow trying out the new frame of reference.
6 Integrating the new frame of reference into daily life and the implications of this.

Both Knowles' theory of andragogy and Mezirow's theory of transformative learning place reflection at the centre of the learning experience. Reflection is crucial to identifying that there is a need for learning: we need to examine previous experiences and frames of reference to understand what we are bringing into the experience and to develop a new way of working moving forward. It is therefore critical that we understand reflection as part of adult learning. One of the most frequently cited models of reflective learning is Kolb's experiential learning cycle.

Kolb's experiential learning cycle

Kolb (1984) developed the experiential learning cycle to explain how experiences translate into learning and behavioural change via reflection. The cycle consists of four different types of learning. In the cycle, concrete experience involves having a direct experience (for example, you receive a low mark on a piece of coursework), which may lead to thoughts and feelings arising (you may be upset). The next stage in the cycle is to reflect on those thoughts and feelings (what has made you feel upset?). Moving to abstract conceptualisation, you then draw conclusions or insights from your reflections that form the basis of more general principles (you come to understand that your grades are very important to your identity as a student) that you can use to self-manage your behaviour moving forward, leading to active experimentation (you will prioritise your studies so you can achieve better grades and feel happier).

Kolb's theory positions learning as a continual process, and it allows us to understand how we move from specific experiences to more general understanding and then test this understanding by altering our behaviour in future situations. One of the benefits of Kolb's cycle is that it can help us to identify what aspect of the learning process we may be weaker in or causes us to get "stuck" and not learn from our experience (Russ, 1998).

Box 5.1 Critique of Kolb

While Kolb's experiential learning cycle is widely used in education, training and organisational contexts across the world, it is not without criticism. Russ (1998) identifies five issues with Kolb's original model:

- It does not take into account social power relations. For example, a black woman experiencing discrimination may be made to think that her experience is not valid, and therefore she cannot learn directly from this experience.
- Sometimes it is better not to learn from direct experience (such as experiencing discrimination) and Kolb's model does not capture how we might learn from the experiences of others.
- The model focuses on looking back at previous experiences, rather than how we can learn from what is happening in the moment.
- **Unconscious** processes and **defence mechanisms** that may form barriers to learning are not accounted for in the model.

> **Unconscious.** Something that an individual is not aware of.

- It does not specify the need to reflect on our process of reflection, without which we may engage in biased reflection processes.

Defence mechanisms. Unconscious processes that protect individuals from painful thoughts and emotions.

Why is it important to coaches?

Learning through reflection is a fundamental part of coaching (Jones, 2021). Helping coachees to engage in reflection enables the coach to facilitate raised awareness in the coachee of what they think, feel, and do. In addition, the coach can help the coachee to explore why their thoughts, feelings, and behaviours are arising. This awareness is needed if coachees are to make conscious choices regarding their future.

Reflection is not straightforward, however. Many coachees will not have engaged in any kind of considered reflection previously and therefore not have the skills to engage in the kind of deep reflective learning outlined in the previous section. It can also be a very difficult process that forces the coachee to confront their own limitations, things they wish they had not done, and situations they wish they had not been in (Jones, 2021). The coach can be there to support the coachee though this difficult process, providing a safe place to explore difficult emotions.

There is considerable evidence to support the use of reflection as a part of learning (Jones, 2021). Evidence of the importance of reflection in coaching is more difficult to establish though, as isolating what outcomes from coaching can be attributed to reflection specifically as opposed to other elements of the coaching process is challenging (e.g., the relationship, goal-setting, etc.). Athanasopoulou and Dopson (2018) conducted a meta-analysis of coaching research and concluded that, while we have a reasonable amount of evidence regarding what outcomes we can expect from coaching, we know very little about how the process of coaching influences these outcomes (i.e., what makes coaching successful or not). There have been some attempts to identify the role reflection plays in coaching. For example, Day and colleagues (2008) explored **critical moments** in coaching (i.e., moments that are seen as significant when looking back at the coaching). They found that when critical moments include reflection, they resulted in a stronger coaching relationship and positive changes for the coachee. When reflection was not present in critical moments, coaches reported that the coaching relationship was damaged.

> **Critical moment.** Moments that are seen as significant when looking back at a coaching session.

Reflection is also seen as a key part of coach development. Grant (2022) discusses how both **reflection on action** (reviewing past coaching sessions) and **reflection in action** (being able to reflect in the moment during a coaching session) are central to a coach being able to learn from their experience and improve their practice. While reflecting on action can be facilitated by coach supervision (Passmore & McGoldrick, 2009), reflection in action requires the development of high levels of **self-awareness** and systems that facilitate this reflection in the moment.

> **Reflection on action.** Thinking deeply about past experiences.
> **Reflection in action.** Thinking deeply about present experiences.
> **Self-awareness.** The ability of an individual to recognise their own thoughts, emotions, and behaviours and how they influence the individual and their interactions with others.

How is this applied in practice?

Knowledge regarding adult learning theories and the importance of reflection to learning is central to effective coaching. Bozer and colleagues (2014) found that when coaches have a background in psychology that includes knowledge of adult development and learning, coaching led to increased self-awareness in coachees. Coach training therefore needs to ensure that coaches have sufficient knowledge of the psychological theories that underpin coaching (see Chapter 2 for further discussion of the need for academic rigour in coach training).

Within a coaching engagement, there are several areas for a coach to pay attention to according to adult learning theories: setting the agenda, providing the right environment, and supporting reflective skills.

Setting the agenda

Ensuring that the agenda for coaching is set by the coachee is central to facilitating adult learning. As discussed earlier in this chapter, adults learn best when the learning relates to real life, there is a need for learning, and it addresses immediate issues in their lives (Knowles et al., 2020). Cox (2015) identifies how this translates into coaching. The coach should ensure that the goal for coaching is always set by the coachee. The coach should also explore what makes the coachee want to focus on this goal. This ensures that the coachee has chosen a goal that has relevance to their life now or an issue that they are currently facing. Coaching tools such as STOKERS (Foy, 2021; see also Chapter 4), where the coach facilitates a discussion of the goal that the coachee wishes to work on, are ideal for ensuring that the coachee focuses on a goal that is meaningful to them. In this stage, open questions such as "What do you want to work on?", "What makes this important to you?", "What difference will this make to you?" can prompt thinking around whether the goal aligns with the principles of adult learning. The coach may also enquire about how the goal aligns with the coachee's values – high alignment with values is likely to result in higher levels of motivation to achieve the goal (Cox, 2015). Kluge and Hageman (2022) summarise that the coach should support the coachee to identify goals that they (the coachee) have the opportunity, time, importance, urgency, and means to achieve.

Providing the right environment

The coaching space can be configured to support reflective thinking in coachees. Some of the most important elements of this include creating time and space for the coachee to engage in what Kahneman (2011) defined as **slow thinking**: a process where we take a more effortful and considered approach to decisions rather than relying on intuition or habit. Having a coaching session provides a dedicated period of

> **Slow thinking.** The process where an individual takes a more effortful and considered approach to decisions rather than relying on intuition or habit.

time for the coachee to think and gives permission for just thinking with nothing else to do. By managing time within the session, the coach takes the stress of time pressure off the coachee, freeing up their ability to engage in slow thinking. By not interrupting, allowing time for silence and allowing the coachee to do most of the talking, the coach also creates the space for the coachee to think more deeply (Kline, 2020).

As outlined above, reflection can be a difficult process that can bring many challenging emotions to the fore. Having a strong and trusting relationship between coach and coachee can make this experience more bearable (Jones, 2021). Hoggan and Kloubert (2020) highlight that for transformative learning to occur the learner needs to feel that their existing perspective is valued and not judged. Therefore, to facilitate reflection the coach needs to pay attention to the quality of the relationship. The person-centred principles outlined in Chapter 3 are all seen as essential to a strong coaching relationship. The coach therefore should aim to hold the coachee in unconditional positive regard, display warmth and empathy, and be genuine, and authentic (DeHaan & Gannon, 2017; Rogers, 1959).

Supporting reflective skills

Reflection does not come naturally to everyone and some people have more developed reflection skills than others (Chivers, 2003; Holden & Griggs, 2011). Evidence suggests that an outcome of coaching is increased self-reflection and self-awareness in coachees (e.g., Bozer et al., 2014; Grant, 2014; Grant et al., 2017; Wales, 2002; Yu et al, 2021). Coaching can promote deeper reflection by orienting coachees towards examining their thoughts, feelings, and behaviours in greater detail than they normally would.

Many of the commonly used models of coaching include elements that can facilitate this reflection. Some of these are summarised in Table 5.1.

Specific coaching approaches have been created to explicitly facilitate reflection. Cox (2013) developed the experiential coaching cycle. This model broadly follows Kolb's cycle, although her focus is on how the coach can facilitate the coachee to move between the stages rather than on the stages per se. It consists of three broad phases in the coaching:

1 Pre-reflection, which consists of everything that the coachee will reflect upon.
2 Reflection on experience, which is the articulation of experiences and the associated thoughts and feelings.
3 Post-reflective thinking, which involves the logical processing of content surfaced in reflection.

Cox (2013) outlines some key skills and techniques that a coach may employ to help a coachee explore and, importantly, transition through these stages. To progress from pre-reflection to reflection on experience, the coachee must be able to recall an experience and access their feelings about it. The coach can support the coachee to access their experiences in numerous ways, including using **visualisation techniques** to recall past events. Cox (2013) suggests that, in the reflection on experience phase, the coachee explores the underlying values,

Visualisation techniques. Mental exercises that involve picturing in detail a past or future scenario.

Table 5.1 Links between coaching approaches and reflection (summarised from Jones, 2021)

Coaching approach	Link to reflection
Behavioural	Exploring current reality in the GROW model prompts reflection on current and past behaviours, thoughts, and feelings. Exploring options invites the coachee to consider how they can apply their learning.
Positive psychology	This includes taking different perspectives, such as zooming in and out, which encourages coachees to challenge the way they view things. For example, the coach may ask the coachee to envisage their best future self in their ideal future without any constraints, and then ask them to zoom out and reflect on the bigger picture.
Systemic coaching	The wider system that the issue sits in can be modelled through techniques such as constellations (see Chapter 6) and reflection facilitated by inviting the coachee to examine the elements in the system and their relationship to one another.
Gestalt coaching	Techniques like the "empty chair" (where the coachee is asked to engage in dialogue with an imagined other in the empty chair, switching places to take on both roles) invite the coachee to take on another perspective and then reflect on what they learn from that position.
Cognitive behavioural coaching	Coachees are invited to take on behavioural experiments to test their assumptions and reflect on their patterns of behaviour. For example, a coachee who has anxiety about public speaking may try speaking in front of a small group, rate their anxiety from 1–10, and gain feedback from the group to test their own assumptions (such as that they are a poor presenter). The coach will then facilitate reflection on the results of the experiment.
Psychodynamic coaching	This facilitates some of the deepest levels of reflection. For example, the coach may share their own emotions with the coachee as they emerge in the coaching session (an example would be that the coach could share that they are feeling defensive in response to what the coachee is saying). This acts as new information for the coachee to reflect upon.

beliefs, prejudices, etc., that underpin their previous experiences. Previous experience is not accepted as is but challenged. She proposes that coaches can use four types of questions to achieve this:

- Lineal questions to gather information about events. For example, "What specific steps did you take to achieve your last goal?"
- Circular questions to explore what the coachee says. For example, "What impact do you believe your decision will have on your family or friends?"
- Strategic questions that relate to "hypotheses" the coach forms. For example, "Given that you often hesitate to take risks, how might embracing a small risk this week help you move closer to your goal?" (where the coach has the hypothesis that taking more risks would benefit the coachee).
- Reflexive questions that allow the coachee to reflect on and reframe their thoughts and beliefs. For example, "How might you view this situation differently if you were to consider it from a friend's perspective?"

Such questions will also help the coachee to move towards post-reflective thinking, where they make sense of the reflective work they have done and what this means for them moving forward. Coachees need to be supported to assimilate their new thinking into their lives, so that there is a change away from the coaching. **Intention strategies**, incorporating techniques such as role play and rehearsal, can help the coachee to prepare for new ways of behaving following their reflections. The coach can also help the coachee to think through their **implementation strategies**, which cover the practicalities of how they are going to implement things in the real world.

> **Intention strategies**. Formulating what changes will be made.
> **Implementation strategies**. Formulating how changes will be made.

Further reading and resources

Ketkin, I. (2023, 7 November). A comprehensive guide to adult learning theories [Post]. The L&D Academy.

Kline, N. (n.d.). *How Can We Enable Our Clients to Think for Themselves?* Henley Business School. Insight Guide #21.

Ragan, T. (2024, February). *The Power of Reflection: How Thinking Improves Learning & Performance – ft. Giada Di Stefano* [Video]. YouTube. https://youtu.be/IRDhHb987Wc?si=FvRztX804z-wkNni.

References

Athanasopoulou, A., & Dopson, S. (2018). A systematic review of executive coaching outcomes: Is it the journey or the destination that matters the most? *The Leadership Quarterly*, *29*(1), 70–88.

Bozer, G., Sarros, J. C., & Santora, J. C. (2014). Academic background and credibility in executive coaching effectiveness. *Personnel Review*, *43*(6), 881–897.

Chivers, G. (2003). Utilising reflective practice interviews in professional development. *Journal of European Industrial Training*, *27*(1), 5–15.

Cox, E. (2013). *Coaching Understood*. Sage.

Cox, E. (2015), Coaching and adult learning: Theory and practice. *New Directions for Adult and Continuing Education, Winter*. 27–38.

Day, A., De Haan, E., Sills, C., Bertie, C., & Blass, E. (2008). Coaches' experience of critical moments in the coaching. *International Coaching Psychology Review*, *3*(3), 207–218.

De Haan, E., & Gannon, J. (2017). The coaching relationship. In T. Bachkirova, G. Spence, & D. Drake (eds), *The SAGE Handbook of Coaching* (pp. 195–217). Sage.

Grant, A. M. (2014). The efficacy of executive coaching in times of organisational change. *Journal of Change Management*, *14*(2), 258–280.

Grant, A. M. (2022). Reflection, note-taking and coaching: If it ain't written, it ain't coaching! *Coaching Practiced*, 71–83.

Grant, A. M., Studholme, I., Verma, R., Kirkwood, L., Paton, B., & O'Connor, S. (2017). The impact of leadership coaching in an Australian healthcare setting. *Journal of Health Organization and Management*, *31*(2), 237–252.

Hoggan, C., & Kloubert, T. (2020). Transformative learning in theory and practice. *Adult Education Quarterly*, *70*(3), 295–307.

Holden, R., & Griggs, V. (2011). Not more learning logs! A research-based perspective on teaching reflective learning within HR professional education. *Human Resource Development International*, *14*(4), 483–491.

Kahneman, D. (2011). *Thinking, Fast and Slow*. Penguin.

Kline, N. (2020). *The Promise That Changes Everything: I Won't Interrupt You*. Penguin.

Kluge, A., & Hagemann, V. (2022). Learning as the basis for coaching. In S. Greif, H. Moller, W. Scholl, J. Passmore, & F. Muller (eds), *International Handbook of Evidence-Based Coaching: Theory, Research and Practice* (pp. 543–552). Springer.

Knowles, M. S. (1980). *The Modern Practice of Adult Education: From Pedagogy to Andragogy* (2nd edition), Cambridge Books.

Knowles. M. (1989). *The Making of an Adult Educator*. Jossey-Bass.

Knowles, M. S., Holton III, E. F., Swanson, R. A., & Robinson, P. A. (2020). *The Adult Learner: The Definitive Classic in Adult Education and Human Resource Development* (9th edition). Routledge.

Kolb, D. (1984). *Experiential Learning*. Prentice Hall.

Lachman, S. J. (1997). Learning is a process: Toward an improved definition of learning. *The Journal of Psychology*, *131*(5), 477–480.

McGrath, V. (2009). Reviewing the evidence on how adult students learn: An examination of Knowles' model of andragogy. *Adult Learner: The Irish Journal Z Adult and Community Education*, *99*, 110.

Mezirow, J. (1997). Transformative learning: Theory to practice. In P. Cranton (ed.), *Transformative Learning in Action: Insights from Practice – New Directions for Adult and Continuing Education*, No. 74 (pp. 5–12). Jossey-Bass.

Mezirow, J. (2000). *Learning as Transformation: Critical Perspectives on a Theory in Progress*. Jossey-Bass.

Mezirow, J., & associates (eds). (1990). *Fostering Critical Reflection in Adulthood*. Jossey-Bass.

Oxford English Dictionary (2024). Learning. https://www.oed.com/search/dictionary/?scope=Entries&q=Learning.

Passmore, J., & McGoldrick, S. (2009). Super-vision, extra-vision or blind faith? A grounded theory study of the efficacy of coaching supervision. *International Coaching Psychology Review*, *4*(2), 145–161.

Rogers, C. R. (1959). A theory of therapy, personality and interpersonal relationships as developed in the client-centred framework. In S. Koch (ed.), *Psychology: A Study of a Science*, Vol. 3: *Formulations of the Person and the Social Context* (pp. 184–256). McGraw-Hill.

Russ, V. (1998). Behind and beyond Kolb's learning cycle. *Journal of Management Education*, *22*(3), 304–319. https://www.proquest.com/scholarly-journals/behind-beyond-kolbs-learning-cycle/docview/195710411/se-2.

Wales, S. (2002). Why coaching? *Journal of Change Management, 3*(3), 275–282.

Yu, N., Collins, C. G., Cavanagh, M., White, K., & Fairbrother, G. (2021). Positive coaching with frontline managers: Enhancing their effectiveness and understanding why. In J. Passmore & D. Tees (eds), *Coaching Researched: A Coaching Psychology Reader* (pp. 269–283). Wiley.

Chapter 6

Theoretical Approaches to Coaching

As discussed in Chapter 1, what distinguishes coaching psychology from coaching is how psychological principles are drawn upon to inform coaching practice. There are many schools of thought within psychology which take very different approaches to understanding human behaviour. Coaching has borrowed from a variety of these approaches, and consequently a variety of psychologically informed approaches to coaching have developed.

This chapter covers four of the main theoretical approaches to coaching: behavioural coaching, cognitive behavioural coaching, psychodynamic coaching, and systemic coaching. Each approach will be outlined, the theoretical background will be discussed, and how it is applied in practice explored.

Behavioural coaching

What is it?

Skiffington and Zeus (2003, p. 6) define behavioural coaching as "A structured, process-driven relationship between a trained professional coach and an individual or team, which includes: assessment, examining values and motivation, setting measurable goals, defining focused action plans, and using **validated** tools and techniques to help coachees develop competencies and remove blocks to achieve valuable and sustainable changes in their professional and personal lives."

Validated. Confirming or verifying that something is accurate and conforms to certain standards.

DOI: 10.4324/9781032686448-8

At its heart, behavioural coaching is about changing behaviours to improve performance. This means that it aligns with many processes in organisations, such as performance-related pay and performance appraisals, making it one of the most sought-after coaching approaches in an organisational context (Eldridge & Dembkowski, 2013).

Behavioural coaching focuses on helping coachees to identify the changes they want to make, understand how their behaviours may be initiated and reinforced by the environment and what the consequences of their behaviours are (Eldridge & Dembkowski, 2013). Effectively, coachees design their own **performance management systems** within behavioural coaching (Passmore, 2019). Most coaching has an element of **behaviourism** in it, typically in setting goals (see Chapter 4 for more on goal-setting).

Performance management systems. Structured frameworks or processes to monitor, assess, and improve employee performance. **Behaviourism/behavioural approaches.** A psychological approach that emphasises the role of the environment on influencing behaviour, including the role of reward and punishment.

What is the underpinning psychology?

Discussions of behaviourism typically start with the work of Pavlov (1927). Pavlov's work with dogs is somewhat legendary in psychology. He observed that when dogs were presented with food they salivated. He experimented with ringing a bell at the same time as presenting food to see if salivation could be produced by the bell alone. Initially, when the bell was rung alone the dogs did not salivate, but after repeated pairings of the bell with the presentation of food, the dogs began to salivate at the sound of the bell alone; they had learned to associate the bell with food. This **associative learning** is the foundation of what became known as **classical conditioning**; we can learn to respond to stimuli based on what we associate with them. For the dogs, they learnt to salivate at the sound of the bell because they were expecting food to follow.

Academics, including Watson (1913), Thorndike (1911) and Skinner (1957, 1974), built upon the ideas of Pavlov and classical conditioning to explore the more volitional behaviours that humans engage in, to encourage the performance of some behaviours, and to reduce the likelihood of others. Often referred to as **operant conditioning**, it explores how the consequences of a certain behaviour impact upon the likelihood of it being repeated. Behaviour that is rewarded in some way is likely to be performed again. This may be through **positive reinforcement** – for example, getting a pay rise for consistently exceeding your sales targets. Alternatively, it may be through **negative reinforcement** – for example, your company removes the threat of redundancies because you have consistently exceeded your sales targets. Behaviour that results in **punishment** on the

Associative learning. A form of learning where an individual learns to associate one stimulus with another, thereby forming a connection between the two.

Classical conditioning. A form of associative learning where the individual learns to associate a neutral stimulus with a stimulus that naturally elicits a response. After repeated pairings, the neutral stimulus alone elicits the response.

Operant conditioning. A form of associative learning where individuals make associations between a behaviour and its consequences.

Positive reinforcement. Pairing a behaviour with a positive consequence, thereby increasing the likelihood of the behaviour being repeated.

Negative reinforcement. Increasing the likelihood of the behaviour being repeated by removing an aversive stimulus.

Punishment. A negative consequence that reduces the likelihood of a behaviour being repeated.

other hand is less likely to be repeated – for example, if you are not included in a reward day out at work because you failed to hit your targets, you will be less likely to miss your targets in future.

Classical and operant conditioning are criticised for not taking into account the complexity of human thought and society (Passmore, 2019). Bandura's (2001) social cognitive theory attempted to integrate these issues into a behaviourist framework. In social cognitive theory, people can learn new behaviours not only from experiencing the pairing of stimuli and reward or punishment themselves, but also from observing the behaviour of others and the consequences of their behaviours. This **vicarious learning** allows us to learn from the successes and failures of others. Bandura also introduced the concept of **self-efficacy**, the belief we have the ability to enact behaviours that will allow us to successfully achieve our goals. Without self-efficacy, we are unlikely to attempt a behaviour, even if we believe that it will lead to rewards or help us avoid punishment.

> **Vicarious learning.** Learning from observing the behaviour, actions, and outcomes of others, particularly the reinforcement or punishment that others receive.
>
> **Self-efficacy.** An individual's belief in their own ability to successfully perform tasks or achieve a goal.

How is this applied in practice?

The most commonly known and used behavioural coaching model is the GROW model (Whitmore, 2017). It was based upon recordings of Graham Alexander's coaching sessions (Alexander & Renshaw, 2005), and was developed and popularised by Sir John Whitmore (2017). It is a structured approach to coaching conversations that takes coachees from setting a goal to developing an action plan, with a clear focus on the coachee's behaviours.

The "G" in GROW stands for goal. In this stage the coach discusses with the coachee what they would like to focus on. The coach then facilitates an exploration of the specific outcomes the coachee is looking for in relation to the topic and how they will know if they achieve those outcomes.

"R" refers to reality. In this stage of the coaching conversation the coach helps the coachee to explore their current situation in order to raise awareness and challenge any assumptions the coachee may be making. The coach can also explore behaviourist principles such as **stimulus control** (Eldridge & Dembkowski, 2013), where things in the environment that make desired or undesired behaviours more likely to occur are identified. Additionally, the coach can enquire about the consequences of the coachee's behaviours to help raise awareness of the reinforcers that serve to increase or decrease the likelihood of those behaviours being repeated.

Stimulus control. When a behaviour is influenced by things in the environment and individuals learn to respond to these stimuli in certain ways.

Under "O" are the options the coachee has explored. The role of the coach for this stage is to help the coachee to explore the full range of options available to them in terms of new behaviours and actions to try, and to evaluate each of these options. The coach can model curiosity and openness here to encourage the coachee to explore options that are beyond their traditional repertoire. The coach can also explore with the coachee what outcomes they might expect from their options and how reinforcing these might be.

"W" is the final stage in GROW is to commit to a way forward or "wrap up". In this stage the coachee moves towards committing to a course of action. They can select at least one of the "options" explored and plan how they will implement that option. Behaviourist principles such as rehearsal – where the coachee can try out a new behaviour in the safety of the coaching relationship, observe the outcomes, and make adjustments accordingly – can be utilised here. Table 6.1 shows some example coaching questions that can be used at each stage of the GROW model.

While GROW has been criticised for being overly simplistic and focused on surface level performance, rather than exploring deeper meanings and drivers for behaviour, it remains the most commonly used approach to coaching (Passmore, 2019).

Table 6.1 Coaching questions within the GROW model

Stage	Example questions
Goal	What do you want to achieve?
	How will you know when you have reached your goal?
	Why is this goal important to you?
	What is the timeframe for achieving this goal?
Reality	What is your current situation regarding this goal?
	What obstacles are you facing?
	How have you addressed similar challenges in the past?
	What resources do you currently have at your disposal?
Options	What are some possible ways to achieve your goal?
	What alternatives can you consider?
	Who else could help you with this?
	What are the pros and cons of each option?
Way forward	What will you commit to doing?
	When will you start taking action?
	How will you hold yourself accountable?
	What might get in your way, and how can you overcome that?

Cognitive behavioural coaching

What is it?

"Cognitive behavioural coaching is an integrative approach which combines the use of cognitive, behavioural, imaginal and problem-solving techniques and strategies within a cognitive behavioural framework to enable coachees to achieve their realistic goals" (Palmer & Szymanska, 2019, p. 108).

Cognitive-behavioural coaching. A coaching approach based on cognitive-behavioural theories that emphasis the link between thoughts, emotions, and behaviour.

Integrative approach. A coaching approach that combines elements from multiple disciplines.

Cognitive behavioural coaching developed from various cognitive behavioural therapies, such as rational emotive behavioural therapy, cognitive therapy, and cognitive behavioural therapy, as well as drawing from approaches focused on problem-solving and solutions (Palmer & Williams, 2013). The crux of all these approaches is the assumption that our feelings are not determined by the events that we experience, but rather by the thoughts we have about these events (Neenan & Dryden, 2020).

What is the underpinning psychology?

The cognitive behavioural approach has its roots in Stoic philosophy and Epictetus, who stated that people are "not disturbed by things but by the view they take of them". Two major theorists in this field are Albert Ellis and Aaron Beck.

Albert Ellis (1962) developed rational emotive behavioural therapy, based upon his ABC model of emotional disturbance. In the ABC model "A" is the activating event, "B" stands for the beliefs we hold about the activating event, and "C" stands for the consequences, including emotions and behaviours. For example, you might be the victim of a scam (A), you believe that people who do this kind of thing are the worst examples of human beings (B), and you feel angry as a result (C). Many people ignore the intermediate role that beliefs play in determining how we feel and respond to something, instead believing that the activating event causes how we feel (e.g., I was scammed and now I am angry). This ignores the fact that different people may have very different beliefs about the event and therefore experience different consequences (Neenan & Dryden, 2020). For example, someone else who is scammed may feel victimised and as a consequence become fearful of online transactions, another person may feel that they could have lost more and therefore feel relieved.

The work of Aaron Beck (1976) focuses on exploring levels of meaning in people's **cognitions**. Beck identified three levels

Cognitions. Thoughts or mental processes.

of cognitions that may need to be identified and explored when helping people to remove emotional disturbances:

1 *Automatic negative thoughts.* These are thoughts that arise without any conscious effort and can be instrumental in determining what we do. For example, if we have the opportunity to take a gap year to travel we might think it's too risky, even before fully exploring the opportunity.
2 *Intermediate beliefs.* These lie beneath the automatic negative thoughts and can be composed of attitudes ("I don't want to be seen as irresponsible"), rules ("I must not do anything too risky") and assumptions ("If I take a risk it will impact badly on my future").
3 *Core beliefs.* These lie at the heart of the issue. They are deep-seated beliefs, often formed early in life, that can be very difficult to change. In this example, the core belief might be "I'm not capable of dealing with risk".

Beck advocated working at whatever level of cognition was needed to evoke change in the client; if the therapist did not need to explore core beliefs and childhood experiences, they would not.

How is this applied in practice?

A key cognitive behavioural coaching model derived from the work of Ellis (1962) is the ABCDE(F) model. This is a **formulation model**; a model where the coach and coachee work together to gain a clear understanding of the issue at hand and how the coachee's behaviours, thoughts, and emotions are connected. As outlined in the previous section, "A" stands for the activating event, "B" for beliefs about that event, and "C"

Formulation model. A model where the coach and coachee work together to get a clear understanding of the issue at hand, and how the coachee's behaviours, thoughts, and emotions are connected.

for the consequences, such as emotions and behaviours. The coach explores the activating event and consequences with the coachee, and then focuses on the beliefs that mediate between the two. This element of the formulation is likely to raise insight in some coachees, who may previously have been unaware of the link between their thoughts and outcomes (Palmer & Szymanska, 2019).

The model then moves on to **disputation** of any irrational or unhelpful thoughts, "D". Taking our earlier example, the coach may explore whether the scammers really are the worst human beings and whether believing this is helpful. The next stage, "E" is deciding upon

Disputation. Challenging an often unhelpful view or belief.

an effective new approach or response. What options does the coachee have to deal with the activating event? What may be more helpful than their previous response? Finally, Palmer (2002) added "F", future focus, to the model; "F" focuses on generating insights from experimenting with "E" that can be integrated into ways of dealing with other issues in the future. In the scam example, our coachee may approach future situations where they have been treated unfairly with curiosity about the perpetrator rather than moving to condemnation and anger.

The "downward arrow" technique is used within the cognitive-behavioural tradition for uncovering underlying assumptions and core beliefs that may be at the root of blockages or negative reactions that coachees are experiencing. Developed by Burns (1990), it involves the coach noticing automatic negative thoughts in the coachee and exploring what such thoughts would mean to the coachee if they were true. Taking our scam example, we may find a coaching conversation using the downward arrow technique could go something like this:

Coachee: They're just the lowest of the low these scammers.
Coach: What if they are, what does that mean to you?
Coachee: Well, it just goes to show that you can't trust anyone can you.

Coach: And if you can't trust anyone, what does that mean
             to you?
Coachee: Well, I can only depend on myself, I'm on my own in
             this world.

Being alone without anyone to depend upon is the core belief in this instance. It may be difficult to shift the automatic negative thoughts without addressing the underlying assumptions and/or core beliefs of the coachee. Once elicited, the coach can work with the coachee to explore whether these assumptions and beliefs are serving the coachee in a positive way, or if there are more helpful ways of thinking they could try.

While the downward arrow technique usually starts with automatic negative thoughts about a particular situation, core beliefs may be impacting many aspects of the coachee's life. For example, in the case of being alone and unable to depend on others the coachee may find delegating at work difficult as well. If core beliefs are shifted, the change can be significant. However, it can be very difficult to shift core beliefs (Padesky, 1994).

Psychodynamic coaching

What is it?

Psychodynamic coaching concerns itself with helping coachees to understand how mental forces operating within and between individuals impact upon the coachee's thinking, feeling, and behaviour

> **Psychodynamic coaching.** A coaching approach that focuses on often unconscious mental forces and how they impact thinking, feeling, and behaviour.

(Roberts & Brunning, 2019). A central idea in psychodynamic coaching is that there are many aspects of mental forces of which we are not consciously aware. Surfacing these unconscious forces can help the coachee to understand what is driving them and enable them to make changes if desired (Lee & Hardingham, 2023).

What is the underpinning psychology?

Psychodynamic theory is based on the work of Sigmund Freud (later developed by his daughter, Anna Freud). Freud's theories are numerous, wide ranging, and vary over the course of his lifetime. Particularly relevant to coaching is the concept of defence mechanisms. Freud suggested that some feelings are too painful or "dangerous" to our self-concept, therefore we push these feelings out of conscious awareness and into our unconscious to protect ourselves (Roberts & Brunning, 2019). This is what is known as a defence mechanism. Table 6.2 details some of the defence mechanisms people employ to protect themselves from unwanted thoughts and feelings.

While defence mechanisms can be healthy and help to protect us, when used excessively they can prevent us from dealing adequately with situations and may set up rigid patterns of unhelpful behaviour, preventing us from reaching our potential (Sandler, 2011; Roberts & Brunning, 2019).

A second relevant psychodynamic theory is object relations theory (Diamond, 2013). Contrary to its name, object relations theory is not about objects in our life, but people. Object relations theory is "concerned with exploring the relationship between real, external people and the internal images and residues of relations with them and the significance of these residues for psychic functioning" (Greenberg & Mitchell, 1983, p. 14). Object relations theory focuses on how our early relationships with our caregivers, with a particular emphasis on mothers, impact on our relationships in the future (Diamond, 2013). If our caregivers are "good enough" then we can form healthy relationships in the future. If early caregiving is inadequate, then dysfunctional relationship patterns may be developed.

Two important concepts for coaching in object relations theory are **transference** and **countertransference**.

Transference. The unconscious redirection of feelings, desires, or expectations from one person onto another person.

Countertransference. A reaction from an individual in response to transference from another individual.

Table 6.2 Defence mechanisms, summarised from Sandler (2011)

Defence mechanism	Description	Example
Denial	Refusing to acknowledge aspects of our emotional experience.	Denying that we are angry with a colleague when they have let us down.
Repression	Burying significant emotional experiences deep in our unconscious.	Having no memory of a traumatic experience in childhood.
Projection	Ascribing a part of ourselves that we do not like to another person, and criticising them.	Criticising a friend for gossiping when we ourselves like to gossip.
Rationalisation	Explaining our actions in logical terms rather than because of emotions.	If we respond angrily to a colleague who criticises us, we may defend this position by claiming that the criticism was unwarranted and any rational person would have felt angry.
Intellectualisation	Explaining away feelings using data or theories.	Using theories of grief to minimise the experience of sadness following a loss.
Splitting	Categorising people or experiences in extreme terms, often viewing them as entirely good or entirely bad.	Seeing achieving a C grade on an essay as a complete failure.
Idealisation	Attributing exaggerated positive qualities to a person and ignoring any negatives.	Seeing a new boss as perfect with no weaknesses.
Denigration	Attributing exaggerated negative qualities to a person and ignoring any positives.	Calling our boss a bad manager and horrible person when they deliver negative feedback to us.

Transference occurs when experiences (often from early life) are brought forward and imposed upon figures in our current life (Roberts & Brunning, 2019). For example, if we experienced a parent who was frequently absent from our lives without explanation, we may react to a partner needing to work abroad with fear and anxiety. In contrast, someone who experienced a parent who was consistently available may react to a partner working abroad in a more benign way. Transference is unconscious and often not communicated directly; the person is unlikely to know that their early relationships are impacting upon their reaction to the present situation and therefore cannot explain to others why they feel the way that they do.

Countertransference refers to a subjective response experienced by the object of transference (Sandler, 2011). For example, the partner in the above example may find themselves reacting with defensiveness and a desire to "escape", to alleviate the discomfort experienced by having an anxious and fearful partner. Again, the countertransference response may be unconscious, as the object of the transference may not be directly aware of how their partner feels nor why they feel the way they do. The early experiences of the object of the transference can impact on their countertransference reactions. For example, having a controlling parent in childhood may trigger an exaggerated desire to "escape" in the above example.

How is this applied in practice?

Psychodynamic coaching is less about tools, techniques, and models and more about the general way the coach approaches the coaching engagement. While not unique to psychodynamic coaching, the coaching relationship is of central importance to the psychodynamic approach to coaching (Sandler, 2011). Psychodynamic coaching aims to develop personal insight by bringing into awareness thoughts and feelings that were previously unknown to the coachee. This can include potentially disturbing and upsetting thoughts and feelings. It is therefore doubly important for the psychodynamic coach to provide a safe environment for the coachee where they can explore these feelings with a non-judgemental coach (Roberts & Brunning, 2019). This can help to contain the unpleasant feelings, making them bearable.

While many coaches strive to minimise the impact of their own emotions in the coaching session, psychodynamic coaches may use their own emotions as sources of data to share with the coachee, with the aim of raising awareness of unconscious emotions in the coachee (Lee, 2010). This requires a high level of self-awareness in a coach, as they have to be able to identify what is arising from their own emotions and what may be a result of countertransference from the coachee. For example, if a coach finds themselves feeling as though they need to rescue a coachee, this could be because they have a need to feel as though they can be helpful *or* because the coachee is transferring a need to have a protector onto the coach.

Psychodynamic coaches may also engage in what Reik (1988) termed "listening with a third ear". This means moving beyond the words of the coachee to examine what is *not* being said. The coach might pay attention to body language, shifts in energy, and shifts in emotion to identify unconscious processes at work in the coachee, and help the coachee explore these. For example, if a coachee becomes very angry or withdrawn in a coaching session, a psychodynamic coach is likely to share that they have noticed this and use open questions to help the coachee explore why that shift in emotion occurred. Again, this is not unique to psychodynamic approaches to coaching, but it is particularly important in the psychodynamic tradition.

Box 6.1 Psychodynamic coaching vs therapy

Arguably one of the "deepest" forms of coaching, psychodynamic coaching runs closer to therapeutic interventions than other theoretical approaches within coaching psychology. Attempting to uncover unconscious patterns from early childhood experiences may be seen as the territory of trained therapists, and while coaches do not offer deep interpretations of unconscious material, they may suggest hypotheses about potential links between the past and present behaviour (Roberts & Brunning, 2019).

Some coaches may not feel suitably skilled to engage in this kind of practice (Lee, 2010), and there is a potential ethical issue if coaches cannot contain the emotional material they surface. While coaches may end up working in the "grey area" with coachees who are experiencing mild symptoms of depression, anxiety, and/or stress, if a coachee becomes incapable of self-management or if the goal of coaching becomes more about exploring deep-seated **trauma** from childhood than personal/professional development, then a referral to psychotherapy is likely needed (Spaten, 2018).

Trauma. Emotional, psychological, or physical response to an event that is considered by the recipient to be deeply distressing or disturbing.

Systemic coaching

What is it?

Senge and colleagues (1994, p. 90) define a **system** as "a perceived whole whose elements 'hang together' because they continually affect each other over time and operate towards a common purpose".

System. A set of interconnected elements that work together as a whole.

Throughout our lives we are all part of multiple systems, starting with our family of origin system and, for most, moving onto educational systems, work systems, community systems, and so on. These systems all have their own explicit and implicit ways of working (Whittington, 2020) and they are interconnected with other systems around them (Hawkins & Turner, 2020). Every person brings with them to coaching not only the systems that they are currently part of, but also every system they have been part of previously (Whittington, 2020).

Whittington (2020, p. 13) defines **systemic coaching** as

Systemic coaching. A coaching approach that focuses on exploring the impact of the coachee's systems on their thoughts, feelings, and behaviour.

coaching that prioritises the system and is informed by an understanding of the organising principles and deep patterns consistently observed in them. This information and perspective are embodied in the inner attitude or "stance" of the coach and shared through the application of systemic questions, interventions, mapping and constellations.

What is the underpinning psychology?

Systemic theories are numerous and complex, not least due to the abstract nature of the principles involved.

One theory that is particularly relevant to coaching is dynamic systems theory. Mahoney (1991) set out to explore how and why people change. A number of systemic principles emerged from his work that can be summarised as follows:

1 Change is a lifelong process, and the rate of change varies at different points in time.
2 Periods of stability in the system result in little change, whereas instability results in more dramatic change.
3 Systems seek stability and stabilising forces maintain patterns of behaviour, even if they are not optimal.
4 Destabilisation is a period of chaos and disorder in the system and is often experienced as being unpleasant by the individual. For example, feeling disoriented, fearful, or as though things are falling apart.
5 For change to occur, there must be destabilisation. Destabilisation can be facilitated by an exploration of the history of the existing system and feeding new information into the system that challenges it.

6 For a new, more adaptive set of patterns to emerge from instability, the individual must have sufficient personal resources and the right environment available, otherwise old patterns or new negative patterns may emerge.

Understanding systemic theories of change can help a coach to explore what forces may be holding a coachee's system stable, what may provoke instability, and how to support the coachee to develop adaptive new patterns.

How is it applied in practice?

One of the most well-known applications of systems theory is Whittington's (2020) coaching constellations. Constellations are a way of exploring the system that the coachee belongs to and the patterns and hidden **dynamics** it contains. Coachees are invited to create a "map" of their system. Representatives (i.e., physical objects) are used to physically "map out" things in the system, including people, events, culture, money, etc. Figure 6.1 shows a constellations map. The circular mat provides a boundary to the system. The objects have different sizes, shapes, and directions of focus that can be used to illustrate the dynamics in the system. The coach asks the coachee to create their map, paying attention to the objects they select, where they place them, direction of focus, and relation to other objects.

> **Dynamics.** Causes or processes that result in change within a system, relationship, or situation.

Once the system has been mapped the coach facilitates an exploration of it. The map is more than a spatial representation of a system – constellations can reveal unconscious patterns, hidden dynamics, and unknown resources that create new insights and ways to move forward. The coachee can experience themselves from an observer position, which leads to fresh information and greater clarity. The coach may ask the coachee to view the map from different places to get different perspectives (e.g., "What

Figure 6.1 An example constellations map.

happens if you move to face the direction your boss is facing?"). The coachee can also be invited to move representatives in the system and see what impact that has on the system. The coach may also offer sentences designed to acknowledge what is in the system or to focus in on the issue more clearly. The overall aim of constellations is to evoke awareness of the issue the coachee is facing from a new perspective, bringing to light awareness of relationships, dynamics, and other perspectives that the coachee may not have previously considered. Insights that emerge from mapping the system and exploring it can then be integrated into the coaching process.

How are the approaches distinguished from one another?

Whilst all coaching psychology approaches follow basic coaching principles – including the coaching being led by the coachee, adoption of a non-judgemental approach, and creating a safe space in which the coachee can share freely – there are some differences in the way that these principles are operationalised within the different theoretical traditions.

Roberts and Jarrett (2006) conducted a piece of research seeking to identify the differences in psychodynamic versus non-psychodynamic approaches. They identified two axes that coaching interventions can differ on. The first axis documents the extent to which the aim of the intervention is focused on goals and outputs versus insight. Behavioural and cognitive behavioural approaches tend to focus on clearly defined goals, improving productivity, and achieving desirable outcomes, whereas psychodynamic and systems approaches tend to focus on generating insights, which may or may not lead directly to performance improvements. The second axis documents whether the intervention focuses on the individual or the organisation. Roberts and Jarrett (2006) identified that behavioural and psychodynamic approaches were focused on the individual, examining personal experiences and emphasising personal responsibility for achievement. Systemic and cognitive behavioural approaches take a wider view, considering the impact of systems that people have belonged to and the interaction between environment and cognition, emotion, and behaviour respectively.

In reality, while some coaching psychologists operate from a purist perspective using one approach to coaching, many coaching psychologists will take an **eclectic approach** to coaching. They draw on different psychological approaches to suit the needs of the coachee they are working with, potentially blending several approaches within a single session (Hardingham, 2021).

> **Eclectic approach.** A coaching approach that combines elements from multiple disciplines.

Further reading and resources

Day, C. (n.d.). The curiosity in cognitive behavioural coaching [Audio podcast episode]. *The AC Podcast*. Association for Coaching.

Krauss Whitborne, S. (2011). *The Essential Guide to Defense Mechanisms*. Psychology Today.

SystemConstellations. (2018, 5 February). Constellations at Henley Business School with John Whittington [Video]. YouTube. https://youtu.be/HWiAMvK4rfA?si=1u2r-CRm75jRQpjS.

The Right Questions. (2021, 8 October). *How to Use the GROW Coaching Model to Achieve Your Goals* [Video]. YouTube. https://youtu.be/D7U0p-JIqcw?si=2QJuRW4sCsOBVplr.

References

Alexander, G., & Renshaw, B. (2005). *Super Coaching*. Random House.

Bandura, A. (2001). Social cognitive theory: An agentic perspective. *Annual Review of Psychology*, 52(1), 1–26.

Beck, A. T. (1976). *Cognitive Therapy and the Emotional Disorders*. International Universities Press.

Burns, D. (1990) *The Feeling Good Handbook*. Plume.

Diamond, M. A. (2013). Psychodynamic approach. In J. Passmore, D. B. Peterson, & T. Freire (eds), *The Wiley-Blackwell Handbook of The Psychology of Coaching and Mentoring*, pp. 365–384. Wiley-Blackwell.

Eldridge, F., & Dembkowski, S. (2013). Behavioural coaching. In J. Passmore, D. B. Peterson, & T. Freire (eds), *The Wiley-Blackwell Handbook of The Psychology of Coaching and Mentoring*, pp. 298–318. Wiley-Blackwell.

Ellis, A. (1962). *Reason and Emotion in Psychotherapy*. Lyle Stuart.

Greenberg, J., & Mitchell, S. A. (1983). *Object Relations in Psychoanalytic Theory*. Harvard University Press.

Hardingham, A. (2021). The universal eclectic model of executive coaching. In J. Passmore (ed.), *The Coaches' Handbook* (pp. 167–175). Routledge.

Hawkins, P., & Turner, E. (2020). *Systemic Coaching; Delivering Value Beyond the Individual*. Routledge.

Lee, G. (2010). The psychodynamic approach to coaching. In E. Cox, T. Bachkirova, & D. Clutterbuck (eds), *The Complete Handbook of Coaching* (pp. 23–36). Sage.

Lee, G., & Hardingham, A. (2023). The psychodynamic approach to coaching. In E. Cox, D. A. Clutterbuck, & T. Bachkirova (eds), *The Complete Handbook of Coaching* (4th edition; pp. 23–35). Sage.

Mahoney, M. J. (1991). *Human Change Processes: The Scientific Foundations of Psychotherapy*. Basic Books.

Neenan, M., & Dryden, W. (2020). *Cognitive Behavioural Coaching: A Guide to Problem Solving and Personal Development*. Routledge.

Padesky, C. A. (1994). Schema change processes in cognitive therapy. *Clinical Psychology & Psychotherapy*, 1(5), 267–278.

Palmer, S. (2002) Cognitive and organizational models of stress that are suitable for use within workplace stress management/prevention coaching, training and counselling settings. *The Rational Emotive Behavior Therapist*, *10*(1), 15–21.

Palmer, S., & Szymanska, K. (2019). Cognitive behavioural coaching: An integrative approach. In S. Palmer, S. & A. Whybrow (eds), *Handbook of Coaching Psychology: A Guide for Practitioners* (pp. 108–130). Routledge.

Palmer, S., & Williams, H. (2013). Cognitive behavioral approaches. In J. Passmore, D. B. Peterson, & T. Freire (eds), *The Wiley-Blackwell Handbook of the Psychology of Coaching and Mentoring* (pp. 319–338). Wiley-Blackwell.

Passmore, J. (2019). Behavioural Coaching. In S. Palmer & A. Whybrow (eds), *Handbook of Coaching Psychology: A Guide for Practitioners* (pp. 99–107). Routledge.

Pavlov, I. (1927). *Conditioned Reflexes.* Oxford University Press.

Reik, T. (1988). The surprised psychoanalyst. In B. Wolstein (ed.), *Essential Papers on Countertransference* (pp. 51–63). New York University Press.

Roberts, V. Z., & Brunning, H. (2019). Psychodynamic and systems-psychodynamics coaching. In S. Palmer & A. Whybrow (eds), *Handbook of Coaching Psychology: A Guide for Practitioners* (pp. 324–340). Routledge.

Roberts, V. Z., & Jarrett, M. (2006). What is the difference and what makes the difference: A comparative study of psychodynamic and non-psychodynamic approaches to executive coaching. In H. Brunning (ed.), *Executive Coaching: Systems-Psychodynamic Perspective.* Karnac.

Sandler, C. (2011). *Executive Coaching: A Psychodynamic Approach.* McGraw-Hill.

Senge, P. M., Kleiner, A., Roberts, C., Ross, R. B., & Smith, B. J. (1994). *The Fifth Discipline Fieldbook: Strategies and Tools for Building a Learning Organization.* Doubleday.

Skiffington, S., & Zeus, P. (2003). *Behavioral Coaching.* McGraw Hill.

Skinner, B. F. (1957). *Verbal Behaviour.* Appleton.

Skinner, B. F. (1974). *About Behaviourism.* Jonathan Cape.

Spaten, O. M. (2018). Visiting the psychotherapy versus coaching psychology conundrum. *Coaching Psykologi*, *7*(1), 7–16.

Thorndike, E. L. (1911). *Animal Intelligence.* Macmillan.

Watson, J. B. (1913). Psychology as the behaviorist views it. *Psychological Review*, *20*(2), 158–177.

Whitmore, J. (2017). *Coaching for Performance: The Principles and Practice of Coaching and Leadership.* NB Publishing.

Whittington, J. (2020). *Systemic Coaching and Constellations: The Principles, Practices and Application for Individuals, Teams and Groups.* Kogan Page.

Section 3

Key Methodologies

This section in summary:

- Quantitative research involves collecting and analysing numerical data.
- Quantitative work typically involves taking a deductive approach to the relationship between theory and data. It is highly structured and is focused on defining and measuring variables; definitions are driven by the researcher and the researcher remains detached from the research.
- Randomised control trials are a form of quantitative research where the researcher randomly allocates participants to groups who either receive the target intervention, another intervention, or nothing; and outcomes are compared.
- Surveys involve collecting data from large groups of people, usually via questionnaires.
- Meta-analyses systematically locate studies in a subject area and use statistical analysis to draw conclusions from that body of knowledge.
- The advantages of quantitative research include its scientific approach and the ability to generalise and establish causal relationships.
- The weaknesses of quantitative research include missing the complexity of human life, assuming the researcher can decide what is important in advance of conducting the research, a lack of ecological validity, biases, and the

DOI: 10.4324/9781032686448-9

problem of trying to measure a bespoke intervention in a standardised way.

- Qualitative research involves collecting and analysing non-numerical data, such as text, images, and videos.
- Qualitative work typically involves taking an inductive approach to the relationship between theory and data, is flexible, is focused on understanding particular cases in depth, uses the language and categories of the participants, and the researcher becomes highly involved in the participants' world.
- In-depth, semi-structured interviews are the most common form of data collection in qualitative research, allowing exploration of participants' experiences.
- Observations can be used to gain direct access to an experience rather than relying on participant recall. The researcher may be actively involved in the situation or a passive observer, and the observation may be overt or covert.
- Systematic literature reviews aim to identify, evaluate, synthesise, and integrate the findings of existing research and are useful in providing an unbiased summary of qualitative and quantitative research conducted to date.
- The strengths of qualitative research lie in its ability to yield rich data and deep understandings of the experiences of participants. It is flexible and allows for new ideas to emerge.
- The weaknesses of qualitative research centre around the specificity of the results to the particular context the research was conducted in, minimising confidence in being able to find the same results with a different set of participants, a different researcher, or at a different point in time.

Chapter 7

Number Crunching

Quantitative Research in Coaching

What are quantitative methods?

In psychology, and therefore in coaching psychology, research is essential to the development of knowledge. Without psychologists having conducted research, there would not be the wealth of evidence-based theories and models we have available today to help us understand how humans behave, instead we would be reliant upon speculation or "common-sense" (Jones et al., in press).

There are many different approaches available to psychologists when they are conducting research. One of the main choices that researchers make is whether they want to conduct what is known as **quantitative research** or **qualitative research**. A rudimentary explanation of what we mean by quantitative versus qualitative is that the terms refer to the type of data collected in the research: quantitative

> **Qualitative research**. Research that involves the collection of non-numerical data.
>
> **Quantitative research**. Research that involves the collection of numerical data.

research involves the collection of numerical data, whereas qualitative research does not. This does not, however, do justice to the different assumptions inherent in these approaches to research.

Rose and colleagues. (2023) identify six ways in which quantitative and qualitative research designs are perceived to differ. In this

DOI: 10.4324/9781032686448-10

chapter we will discuss the characteristics of quantitative designs in relation to these six characteristics. In Chapter 8 we will discuss qualitative designs. As indicated above, the first difference relates to the kind of data that are collected. Quantitative studies collect numerical data with the aim of being able to perform statistical analyses that allow us to make **inferences** from the sample we study to a wider population. For example, if we study 100 experienced coaches, we assess the extent to which our results may apply to all experienced coaches. The second characteristic of quantitative research is that there tends to be what is known as a deductive relationship between theory and research. When taking a **deductive approach** to research, the researcher will start with reading existing theory and developing predictions, known as **hypotheses**, from this. The data are then collected to test these hypotheses. In short, existing theory precedes data. Third, quantitative designs are typically very structured. What will happen, when, and with whom are all decided in advance and these procedures are adhered to. Any deviations from this can be seen as a weaknesses of the study. Fourth, quantitative researchers typically seek to identify variables (characteristics or concepts upon which the sample can vary) and establish how to measure these in a consistent way prior to commencing the research. Fifth, quantitative researchers adopt what is known as the **etic approach**, where the researcher defines

> **Inferences**. Applying conclusions from data collected from one sample to the wider population.
>
> **Deductive approach**. An approach to research where the researcher develops and tests predictions from existing theory.
>
> **Hypotheses**. A testable statement of the relationship between two or more variables or differences among groups based on prior knowledge, observations, or theory.
>
> **Etic approach**. An approach to research where the researcher defines the concepts and their boundaries in advance of collecting data.

the concepts they are interested in and the boundaries of these in advance of collecting data. Participants have no say in what is studied and how it is defined. Finally, in quantitative research the researcher typically seeks to stay objective, minimise their impact on the situation they are studying, and control as many aspects of the situation as possible, to increase their confidence in the conclusions drawn from the data. This is often associated with what is known as a **positivist** philosophical position. Positivists assume that there is an **objective reality** and the best way to find out about this reality is to research it as objectively as possible (Oades et al., 2019).

> **Positivist**. A philosophical position that assumes an objective reality and advocates the use of objective research methods.
> **Objective reality**. Assumption that the world around us is independent of people and their interpretations of it.

The next section will demonstrate how these characteristics can be seen in three of the main types of quantitative research employed in coaching psychology: randomised control trials, surveys, and meta-analyses.

Quantitative methods in action

Randomised control trials

Randomised control trials are seen as the "gold standard" of **empirical research** that can be conducted by psychologists (Fillery-Travis & Collie, 2019). Randomised control trials are a kind of **experimental research**, where the researcher manipulates the participants'

> **Empirical research**. Research that involves the collection of data.
> **Experimental research**. A type of research that seeks to investigate cause and effect by manipulating the participants environment in some way.

environment in some way to see what happens. In coaching psychology research, this manipulation is usually the provision of a coaching intervention.

Imagine that we are interested in seeing whether coaching that incorporates the use of metaphor improves people's level of creativity. We could find a sample of people, measure their level of creativity with a questionnaire that we know has been shown to assess levels of creativity (more on this in the next section), give them the coaching intervention using metaphors, and then test their levels of creativity afterwards with the same questionnaire to see if there is any difference in their creativity scores. If their scores go up, we could conclude that coaching with metaphors improves a coachee's creativity. There are several problems with this conclusion though (Oades et al., 2019). The main issue is that we cannot infer causality from this kind of research: we might find that creativity scores did go up for the participants, but we cannot be sure that is because of the coaching intervention. It may be that people's scores naturally increase over time, it could be that completing a questionnaire on creativity made people focus on creativity and increase the number of creative hobbies they did, or that unknown to us our participants all participated in a creative writing course over the duration of the study. To be able to make claims about whether there is an impact from an intervention, we need to be able to compare what happens in a group of people who receive the intervention with what happens in a group of people who do not receive the intervention, known as the **control group** (Oades et al., 2019).

Control group. A group in an experimental research study that does not receive the experimental treatment or intervention being tested.

This is an experimental design and is visualised in Figure 7.1.

However, just having a control group is not sufficient to infer causality. You need to be able to demonstrate that there are no systematic differences (in characteristics or experiences over the course of the intervention) between the group that receive the intervention (often known as the experimental or intervention group) and the control group (Oades et al., 2019). One of the key

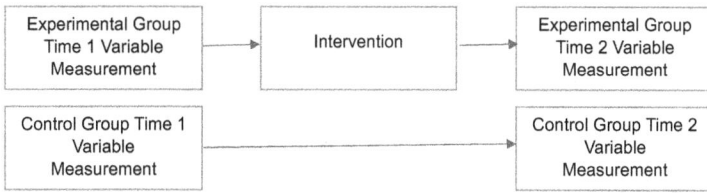

Figure 7.1 Experimental design.

ways of doing this is to randomly allocate participants to the experimental and control groups. With a sufficiently large **sample** size, this random allocation should reduce the possibility of systematic differences between the two groups. It is known as a randomised control trial (RCT; Rose et al., 2023). Where it is not possible (or desirable) to allocate participants to groups randomly then the study is known as a **quasi-experimental design**.

Sample. The people who take part in a research study.

Quasi-experimental design. An experimental design where participants are not randomly allocated to groups.

Box 7.1   Quasi-experimental designs

Quasi-experimental designs have an experimental group and a control group, but participants are not randomly allocated between the two groups (Rose et al., 2023). Non-random allocation of participants means that we cannot rule out that differences between the experimental group and control group are not due to the intervention, but some other difference between the groups.

Randomised control trials are not always possible for a number of reasons. In coaching research in particular, only offering coaching (which we believe is going to be beneficial) to some of our participants and not others, could be seen as unethical. In our study of the impact of coaching students on their ability to secure a work placement (Andrews & Jones, 2024) we used a quasi-experimental design for this very reason. We did not want to disadvantage students in their search for a work placement by denying them coaching if they wanted it, therefore we coached all students who wanted coaching and they formed the experimental group and compared them with students who were registered to take a work placement but did not want coaching as the control group.

To draw conclusions from our work, we needed to be able to rule out alternative explanations for any increases in the likelihood of securing a placement for the experimental group. We therefore checked the **demographic characteristics** of the participants in both groups to ensure there were no differences.

> **Demographic characteristics.** The characteristics of participants within a research group (e.g., age, gender, ethnicity, etc.).

We found that males were more likely to be coached, and therefore we controlled for gender in our analyses to remove the impact of this (known as a confounding variable). We hypothesised that levels of commitment to securing a work placement might differ between the two groups, with those opting for coaching being more committed, but we did not find a significant difference between the groups on commitment. Finally, we checked to see if the participants in the two groups differed in terms of their self-efficacy, but again there were no significant differences. By performing these checks and controlling for gender, we could be more confident that our results were due to the coaching intervention, but we could not rule out other confounding factors that we did not measure.

Recently, people have begun to question the usefulness of having control groups that do nothing at all (Oades et al., 2019). Doing something will often out-perform doing nothing, and therefore a comparison between a group who receive an intervention and a group who do not, does not always tell us a lot about how useful this intervention is in comparison with other things we could have done. Instead (or in addition to a standard control group), you

Active control group. A group in an experimental research study that receives an alternative intervention to the one being tested.

may have what is known as an **active control group**. Looking at our earlier example of wanting to assess whether coaching using metaphors improves creativity, if we found that creativity increased in the experimental group but not the control group we could conclude that this was due to the intervention. However, we do not know what about the intervention caused the increase. Was it the metaphors specifically, or would any coaching have improved creativity? To address this question, we could also include an active control group in our design where the participants receive coaching without metaphors. If we found a difference between this group and our coaching with metaphor group we could be more confident that the addition of metaphors to coaching was having the impact. This type of design is visualised in Figure 7.2.

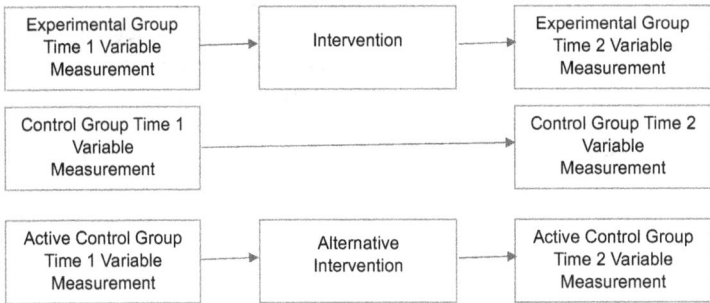

Figure 7.2 An experimental design with control group and active control group.

An emerging research area where RCTs have been used is AI in coaching. Terblanche and colleagues (2022) compared two randomised control trial studies that measured the increase in coachee goal attainment after receiving coaching over a 10-month period. One study involved human coaches and the other study used an AI chatbot coach. All participants in both studies were undergraduate students at a UK business school.

In study one, participants were coached by profession-ally trained coaches with a minimum of three years coaching experience. In study two, an AI coach named Vici was used. Vici is a text-based chatbot designed to assist participants with goal-achievement. This includes helping users to identify goals, define actions to reach the goals, monitor progress, and adjust if necessary. Vici also helps users to differentiate between prox-imal, process, and distal goals, on the one hand, and end and dream goals on the other, and keeps track of both. In both studies, participants were more likely to reach their goals work-ing with human coaches and the AI coach compared to the two control groups.

The authors report that the AI coach was as effective as human coaches at the end of the trials. However, there is an issue with drawing this conclusion from two separate RCTs. Whenever we want to test the effectiveness of an intervention compared to another intervention (e.g., human coaching compared to AI coaching) or compared to no intervention (e.g., AI coaching compared to no coaching), we must include all participants in the same study so that we can test whether there are any signifi-cant differences between the groups. Whilst it can be helpful to compare the findings from different studies to consider the impli-cations of these findings for practice, unless we have tested for significant differences within a randomised controlled trial – in this case with three conditions in the same experiment (condi-tion 1 = human coaching, condition 2 = AI coaching, and condi-tion 3 = no coaching) – we cannot draw accurate conclusions on whether AI coaching is as effective as, less effective than, or more effective than human coaches.

Surveys

The **survey strategy** in research design involves collecting data from a group of people. This is often a large group of people, with the aim of **generalising** the results to the population from which the sample were selected (Saunders et al., 2023). **Questionnaires** are one of the most common ways that data

Survey strategy. A research design that involves collecting data from (a usually large) group of people.
Generalising. Inferring conclusions drawn in relation to one or more samples from the wider population.
Questionnaires. A data collection method that involves presenting the same set of questions to all participants.

are collected within the survey strategy (Saunders et al., 2023). Indeed, the two are so connected that the terms survey and questionnaire are often used interchangeably, but this is not accurate. Survey is the strategy adopted and questionnaire is the data collection method. The survey strategy could also use other data collection methods, such as observations or even interviews (although this would be very time consuming) and questionnaires can be used in other research strategies too, such as experiments.

Questionnaires can be defined as a set of questions or items presented to participants with the intention of capturing information about attitudes, feelings, behaviours, demographics, etc. (Clark et al., 2021). While questionnaires can include open-ended questions, and therefore capture qualitative data, they are most often used to collect quantitative data (Saunders at al., 2023). Often, questionnaires are designed with a response format known as a **Likert scale** (Jones et al., in press). Likert scales ask people to indicate their response to an item or question on a rating

Likert scale. A format often used in questionnaires which typically presents a statement, and respondents are asked to indicate their level of agreement on a multipoint scale.

scale. For example, we could ask people how much they agree with the statement: "My coach really cared about me" on a scale from 1 (strongly disagree) to 5 (strongly agree). This would be a Likert scale item.

When we are planning on using questionnaires in a survey study, one of the key things that we need to do is to identify what we are interested in finding out about and how we are going to measure it (Rose et al., 2023). This involves defining the key **variables** or concepts that we wish to investigate and then identifying how we might assess this within a questionnaire. Typically, we seek to find existing measures of the variables that we are interested in and use these within our questionnaire. For example, if we wanted to examine generalised self-efficacy in a study, we might choose to include the questions from Chen and colleagues' (2001) generalised self-efficacy scale in the study.

> **Variables.** Anything that can be measured, manipulated, or controlled in a research study.

When selecting what measures to include in a questionnaire, the **reliability** and **validity** of those measures are extremely important as markers of the quality of the results we can expect. Reliability refers to the consistency of the results and validity refers to the extent that we are measuring what we are purporting to measure (Saunders et al., 2023).

> **Reliability.** The consistency or dependability of a measurement or instrument.
> **Validity.** The degree to which an instrument or study measures what it is intending to measure.
> **Validation study.** A piece of research which seeks to establish the reliability and validity of a measure.

There are several ways to assess the level of reliability and validity of a measure. First, most measures have what is known as a **validation study** published, which provides details of how the scale was created and its reliability and validity. The Chen and colleagues' (2001) paper referred to above is an example of a validation study. Second, the extent to which the measure has been used in other published studies and the results that have been found using that measure can be assessed. If we can see that a measure has been successfully used a high number of times in our

Table 7.1 Types of reliability and validity summarised from Saunders et al. (2023)

Metric	Description
Content validity	The extent to which the measure adequately covers the concept or variable of interest.
Criterion-related (predictive) validity	The extent to which the measure can make accurate predictions about other, theoretically related, variables.
Construct validity	The extent to which the measure reflects the underlying variable it purports to measure. Convergent and discriminant validity are types of construct validity.
Convergent validity	The extent to which scores on the measure overlap with scores on other measures of the same variable.
Discriminant validity	The extent to which scores on the measure do not overlap with scores on measures of different variables.
External/ecological validity	The extent to which scores on the measure generalise to the real world.
Internal consistency reliability	The extent to which items in the measure "hang together". If someone scores highly on one item they should theoretically score highly on the other items in the measure (if all the items measure one construct). Cronbach's alpha coefficient is the most frequently reported statistic assessing this. Scores can fall between 0 and 1, with 0.7 or above being seen as acceptable.
Alternate form reliability	The extent to which the same results are found when using alternative versions of the questions included in the measure.
Test-retest reliability	The extent to which participants get the same scores if tested on more than one occasion.
Inter-rater reliability	The extent to which different researchers achieve similar results, if the measure is administered by the researcher.

subject area, then it could be assumed that it likely has good levels of reliability and validity.

When you read validation studies you will likely come across many technical terms related to reliability and validity. Table 7.1 provides an overview of some of the different kinds of reliability and validity you might read about.

In coaching research, many phenomena have been investigated via questionnaires. For example, Gan and colleagues (2021) investigated factors that impacted the effectiveness of coaching in Malaysia. A total of 600 questionnaires were sent to employees who had received coaching by an International Coach Federation (ICF) accredited coach, with 320 questionnaires returned. The questionnaires included measures of coaching effectiveness, coachee characteristics (proactivity, goal orientation, feedback receptivity), the quality of the coaching relationship (rapport with the coach, trust, and commitment), coach-centric constructs (coach personality, credibility, and skills), and organisational support. The results showed that organisational support, coachee characteristics, and relationship quality significantly influence coaching effectiveness, with organisational support being the most crucial factor. One criticism of this paper is that the specific measures included in the questionnaire are not specified, therefore the reliability and validity of the results cannot be judged.

Meta-analysis

The research approaches and data collection methods we have reviewed so far have focused on data that are created as part of the research process. These data are known as **primary data** (Rose et al., 2023). Researchers can also use data that already exists independent of the research process. These data are known as **secondary data** (Rose et al., 2023). One method of using existing data is to conduct what is known

Primary data. Data that are created and collected as part of the research process.
Secondary data. Data that exist independently of the research process.

as a meta-analysis. A meta-analysis is "the statistical synthesis of results from a series of studies" (Borenstein et al., 2009, p. xxi) and it is a particularly useful technique as it allows the researcher to systematically review a whole body of research evidence and draw conclusions (based on statistical analysis), permitting the researcher to determine objectively the effect of the intervention being examined.

Meta-analysis is concerned with **effect sizes**. Effect sizes tell us about the practical importance of our results. With large samples, it is possible to find a statistically significant difference between groups or relationship between variables that have very little practical significance (i.e., the actual difference between the groups is minimal or the relationship is weak; Saunders et al., 2023). Most coaching practitioners would hope that their coaching intervention generated a large improvement in outcomes for the coachee, and, in research terms, this would translate into a large effect size. Meta-analysis allows us to examine the consistency of an effect size across lots of studies, in different samples, possibly generated using different procedures. If a consistent effect size is found, then we can be more confident that results are robust across a range of contexts. If we find differences in effect sizes then we can potentially establish what factors or **moderators** may influence the impact (Borenstein et al., 2009). The other benefit of using meta-analytic techniques is that the researcher can "control" for other factors that can influence results from research – for example, small sample sizes and reliability of outcome measures.

> **Effect size**. A measure of the practical importance of statistical analyses.
>
> **Moderators**. Variables that alter relationships between other variables.

A natural progression in a discipline is that as the body of research grows, so too do the number of meta-analyses. This is exactly what we are witnessing in the field of coaching. For example, a recent meta-analysis conducted by Wang and colleagues (2021) examined how outcomes from coaching differ according to the coaching approach used. The authors compared four different coaching methods: GROW, cognitive-behavioural coaching, positive psychology coaching, and integrative coaching (where several coaching approaches were applied, including cognitive-behavioural coaching and solution-focused coaching). They found that each coaching approach had positive effects on coaching outcomes, with no one approach producing better results than another. The authors argue that this result is aligned with "outcome equivalence" in therapeutic research, which shows that there is no significant difference in effectiveness between different therapeutic approaches and techniques. They argue that their findings contribute to the debate on coaching approaches by suggesting that no approach is superior to another.

As the body of literature in coaching increases, researchers can be more discerning in their selection of studies for inclusion and exclusion in meta-analyses. DeHaan and Nilsson (2023) conducted a meta-analysis on the effectiveness of coaching using only randomised control trials. They identified 37 RCT studies published between 1994 and 2021 for inclusion in their meta-analysis. They found that overall, coaching had a significant impact on all leadership and personal outcomes identified, with a moderate effect size. They also identified some aspects of the coaching engagement that impacted upon the strength of the effect size shown: stronger effects were found for self-reported outcomes as opposed to objectively assessed ones; qualified coaches not in leadership positions achieved stronger outcomes for coachees; and female coachees achieved better outcomes than the male coachees. The length of the coaching relationship did not impact on the strength of the effect. The authors assert that this study provides clear evidence of the efficacy of coaching in a variety of situations.

As the field of coaching research continues to develop, meta-analyses have an important role to play in building our knowledge and understanding of what works in coaching (however, see Chapter 2 for a critique of relying solely on this kind of evidence). So far, we know that coaching appears to have a positive impact on many different types of outcomes, that the working alliance is significantly related to outcomes, and that all coaching approaches appear equally effective.

Strengths of quantitative research

Quantitative research in social sciences, including coaching psychology, tries to assume many of the characteristics of "scientific" research (Saunders et al., 2023). The scientific approach has various strengths. First, the researcher is seen as being more objective in quantitative work, not imposing their own interpretations onto data, but instead being on the outside of the research process (Oades et al., 2019). This is related to the second principle of **replicability** (Oades et al., 2019). Because quantitative work involves highly structured, standardised procedures and the impact of

Replicability. The ability to repeat research and obtain the same results.

the researcher is minimised, it should therefore be possible to repeat the work and obtain the same results. Taking a scientific approach also allows quantitative researchers the possibility of generalising their results from the sample studied to a wider population. With its focus on large sample sizes and use of statistical techniques to assess whether the results found in a sample are likely to be found in the population, this ability to generalise is seen as strength of quantitative work (Oades et al., 2019; Rose et al., 2023).

Depending on the type of research design adopted within quantitative research, we may be more able or less able to establish **causation** based upon the results (Oades et al., 2019). Experimental designs are particularly strong in this regard (Rose et al., 2023). Being able to establish causality is important in coaching research: coaches want

Causation. The relationship between at least two variables where one variable directly influences or causes a change in another.

to be confident that their work is having a positive impact on coachees and buyers of coaching wish to ensure that the money they invest in coaching is well spent.

Weaknesses of quantitative research

There are a number of general weaknesses of quantitative research. One of the main criticisms of this kind of work is that it is reductionist: it reduces incredibly complex human behaviour into numbers. In doing this we lose much of the richness and under-standing of what is hap-

> **Reductionist**. Breaking down complex phenomena into simpler components.

pening for participants and why (Oades et al., 2019). Linked to this, by focusing on transforming complex phenomena into neat, numerical data, we necessarily have to narrow down the focus of our research to a very specific question, which may exclude lots of other potentially important variables (Oades et al., 2019). We also define what variables we are going to focus on in advance of col-lecting our data, so we miss the opportunity to gain new insights from participants (Oades et al., 2019).

Although some of the strengths of quantitative research relate to the ability to demonstrate the validity of the conclusions we are drawing, one area of validity where quantitative work may be lacking is ecological validity (i.e., the extent to which our findings apply to the real world) (Oades et al., 2019). Particularly with experiments, to be confident that the intervention is having an impact, we may set up an artificial situation where other potential influences are eliminated. Such a situation is unlikely to happen in the real world and therefore the results we find via a controlled experiment may not be found when we implement the intervention in an organisation, for example. The validity of quantitative work may also be threat-ened by various biases. Notably, **response bias** is often an issue in this kind of work: people voluntarily choose to be part of research and there may be some-

> **Response bias**. Systematic ten-dency of respondents to provide inaccurate answers.

thing different about those people as opposed to the people who do not choose to take part (Rose et al., 2023). It may be that those who volunteer have particularly strong opinions on the sub-ject we are interested in or have more direct experience in the area than most. Because we cannot access those who do not choose to take part, we cannot know what these differences are. Quantitative work is also susceptible to social desirability bias, where participants tell the researcher what they think the researcher wants to hear or answer in such a way as to present themselves in a positive light (Rose et al., 2023). This can be a particular issue in coaching research, as coaches may be motivated to present their own work in a positive light and coachees may feel that they have to respond positively about coaching because, for example, they like their coach, they have invested a lot of time in the process, or because it has cost a lot of money.

There are some particular weaknesses of quantitative work in coaching psychology. One of the biggest advantages of coaching as a learning and development tool is that the coachee leads and directs the focus of the coaching conversation. This means that the coachee can tailor the support they receive based on their needs. In research, this is where the problem arises: if each coachee has a different set of requirements and a different set of goals they seek to achieve, how can we evaluate the impact of coaching in a way that is consistent across multiple coachees, coaches, and contexts? In narrowly defining what variables the research is going to focus on, the quantitative researcher may not fully capture the coaching experience for all coachees and coaches.

Further reading and resources

Bhandari, P. (2022, 6 May). *Questionnaire Design: Methods, Question Types & Examples*. Scribbr. https://www.scribbr.co.uk/research-meth ods/questionnaire-design/.

Jones, R. J. & Andrews, H. (2021, 19 August). Walk and talk coaching (No. 41) [Audio podcast episode]. *The Coaching Academic*. Apple Podcasts. https://podcasts.apple.com/gb/podcast/ep-41-walk-and-talk-coaching/id1321572986?i=1000532489635.

Saunders, M. (2024, 9 September). Mark Saunders on Research Methods, *Quantitative Research Designs and the Research Onion* [Video]. YouTube. https://youtu.be/IqgAjKyPuTk?si=d36UH9vvo1E6hBSc.

References

Andrews, H., & Jones, R. J. (2024). Can one-to-one coaching improve selection success and who benefits most? The role of internship candidate generalised self-efficacy. *Coaching: An International Journal of Theory, Research and Practice*, 1–16.

Borenstein, M., Hedges, L. V., Higgins, J. P., & Rothstein, H. R. (2021). *Introduction to Meta-Analysis*. Wiley.

Chen, G., Gully, S. M., & Eden, D. (2001). Validation of a new general self-efficacy scale. *Organizational Research Methods*, 4(1), 62–83.

Clark, T., Foster, L., Bryman, A., & Sloan, L. (2021). *Bryman's Social Research Methods*. Oxford University Press.

DeHaan, E., & Nilsson, V. O. (2023). What can we know about the effectiveness of coaching? A meta-analysis based only on randomized controlled trials. *Academy of Management Learning & Education*, 22(4), 641–661.

Fillery-Travis, A., & Collie, S. (2019). Research and the practitioner: Getting a perspective on coaching psychology research. In S. Palmer & A. Whybrow (eds), *Handbook of Coaching Psychology: A Guide for Practitioners* (2nd edition). Routledge.

Gan, G. C., Chong, C. W., Yuen, Y. Y., Yen Teoh, W. M., & Rahman, M. S. (2021). Executive coaching effectiveness: Towards sustainable business excellence. *Total Quality Management & Business Excellence*, 32(13–14), 1405–1423.

Jones, S., Forshaw, M., Steele, C., & Andrews, H. (in press). *Research Methods and Statistics in Psychology*. Pearson.

Oades, L., Siokou, C. L., & Slemp, G. (2019). *Coaching and Mentoring Research: A Practical Guide*. SAGE.

Rose, S., Spinks, N., & Canhoto, A. I. (2023). *Management Research: Applying the Principles of Business Research Methods*. Routledge.

Saunders, M. K., Lewis, P., & Thornhill, A. (2023). *Research Methods for Business Students* (9th edition). Pearson.

Terblanche, N., Molyn, J., de Haan, E., & Nilsson, V. O. (2022). Comparing artificial intelligence and human coaching goal attainment efficacy. *PloS One, 17*(6).

Wang, Q., Lai, Y. L., Xu, X., & McDowall, A. (2021). The effectiveness of workplace coaching: A meta-analysis of contemporary psychologically informed coaching approaches. *Journal of Work-Applied Management*, 14(1), 77–101.

Chapter 8

The Devil is in the Detail
Qualitative Research in Coaching

What are qualitative methods?

In Chapter 7 we introduced one distinction that is made when conducting research: whether the data collected are quantitative or qualitative. We discussed the characteristics of quantitative data in Chapter 7, and in this chapter we will explore qualitative data. Qualitative data can be anything that is non-numerical including words, images and videos (Saunders et al., 2019).

Rose et al. (2023) cover six ways in which qualitative data differs from quantitative data. Here, we will explore the characteristics of qualitative data and you should refer to Chapter 7 for a discussion of quantitative data. First, qualitative research involves the collection of non-numerical data. As mentioned above, this can take many forms, but it is primarily in the form of text. When analysing qualitative data, researchers do not make use of statistical techniques and instead focus on making sense of the data they collect through **coding** the data and generating themes from those codes. Second, qualitative work is generally associated with an **inductive** relationship between theory and data. This means that rather than starting with a theory and collecting data to test that theory, data are collected first and theory is built from that data. In short, data precedes theory. Third, qualitative designs are often

Coding. The process of organising and categorising qualitative data into meaningful themes.
Inductive. An approach to research that begins with data from which theory is built.

DOI: 10.4324/9781032686448-11

flexible; the researcher is able to respond to what is emerging from the data and make changes to the design of the study in the moment. Fourth, the work focuses upon cases (usually participants) rather than variables. The researcher does not necessarily have a clear idea of what variables or concepts they may be expecting to be relevant to the study and they certainly have not established a standardised way of measuring any variables across participants. Instead, qualitative researchers are interested in the uniqueness of individual cases. Fifth, the **emic approach** to concept specification is often adopted in qualitative work, where the researcher seeks to understand the views of the participants, rather than impose a predefined conceptualisation onto participants. Finally, qualitative researchers often aim to become deeply involved in the world of the participants to fully understand their experiences and perspectives in as natural a situation as they can. This is associated with what is known as an **interpretivist** philosophical position, where the assumption is that everyone has their own interpretation of reality and that we should be aiming to understand our participants' individual realities as accurately as possible (Oades et al., 2019). Some qualitative work goes further still and asserts that we cannot "accurately" know about another person's reality, as the very act of investigating that reality changes things, therefore our research should be aiming to understand what happens in our exchanges with participants – this view is associated with a **social constructionist** philosophical position (Rose et al., 2023).

Emic approach. An approach to research where the researcher seeks to understand phenomena from the participant's perspective.
Interpretivist. A philosophical position that assumes that reality is subjective and constructed by the individual.
Social constructionist. A philosophical position that assumes that reality is constructed through social interactions.

The next section will explore how interviews and observations can be used to collect qualitative data, and how qualitative research findings can be analysed using systematic literature reviews.

Qualitative methods in action

Interviews

Brinkman and Kvale (2015) describe qualitative research **interviews** as "attempts to understand the world from the subjects' point of view, to unfold the meaning of their experience, to uncover their lived world" (p. 3). Interviews that seek this kind of rich understanding are known as in-depth interviews (Rose et al., 2023). In research, these kinds of interviews are typically conducted in what is known as a **semi-structured interview** format, where the researcher has some predetermined questions that they would like to ask the participants, but they can also ask other follow-up questions, ask for more detail, or explore new avenues prompted by the participants'

> **Interview.** A data collection method where the researcher asks an individual or group a series of questions designed to gather in-depth information.
> **Semi-structured interview.** An interview that combines a set of predefined questions with the flexibility to explore participant responses.

responses (Saunders et al., 2023). The questions to be asked are based upon the research questions of the study, the researcher's review of the literature, their prior experience, or discussions with knowledgeable others (Rose et al., 2023). Interviews can also be fully structured, where all participants are asked the same questions in the same order, or unstructured, where there are no predetermined questions (Saunders et al., 2023).

When conducting interviews, finding the right people to interview is key. Those you select as participants need to have the relevant knowledge or experience in the subject area you wish to explore in order to supply useful data (Oades et al., 2019). For example, if you wish to research what it means to be a climate-conscious coach, then you need to interview a sample of coaches who identify as being climate conscious.

Interviewers also need to consider the logistics of conducting interviews. One big decision is whether to conduct interviews on a one-to-one basis, or to do group interviews. One-to-one interviews are best suited to when you wish to explore individual experiences in depth, whereas group interviews can be useful when you wish to explore topics that benefit from discussion in a social setting and where participant inputs may spark ideas in other participants (Rose et al., 2023).

Another decision is whether to conduct interviews face-to-face or via technology. While face-to-face interviews can be good for building trust and rapport with participants, interviews conducted via telephone or using video-conferencing technology can allow researchers to interview more geographically diverse participants and are more convenient and economical to conduct (Oades et al., 2019). Interviews can also be conducted asynchronously using email or messaging software. This may be particularly useful for very sensitive topics where the participant may not want to meet with the interviewer directly (Rose et al., 2023).

Interviews are usually recorded and then transcribed to give a written account of the interview. This is then analysed by the researcher. One of the most common methods of analysing qualitative interview data is using **thematic analysis**, a "method for identifying, analysing and interpreting patterns of meaning ('themes') within qualitative data" (Clarke and Braun, 2017, p. 297). Thematic analysis includes six steps:

> **Thematic analysis**. A process to analyse qualitative data with a focus on extracting themes.

1 Familiarise yourself with the data.
2 Attach codes to "chunks" of data that appear pertinent to the research question, so as to identify and describe those chunks.
3 Search for themes (which are patterns within the codes) that are meaningful for your research question.
4 Review potential themes.
5 Define and name themes.
6 Produce a report of the study.

Interviews can be particularly useful to explore relatively new areas of a discipline. As an example in coaching, Quinn and colleagues (2022) compared the experiences of five participants after they participated in a one-to-one coaching intervention that included the use of Lego, a relatively new technique within coaching. While Lego is usually seen as a toy, it can be used in coaching to help coachees explore problems creatively, visualise their situation or goals, and break down complex decisions. Participants were interviewed immediately after receiving coaching. The researchers identified three themes from the data: creating awareness and new insights, time to think, and emotional security. Participants stated that the Lego changed their thinking processes and released thoughts and feelings. The researchers found that introducing Lego freed up more time to think, by slowing down the coaching process and enabling participants to let go of preconceived ideas. This led to changes in thought patterns for participants and a deeper level of understanding to the thought process. The researchers also reported that participants experienced emotional security from using Lego, with play being a contributing factor. They suggest that the sense of safety came from linking play to their own childhood experiences and experiences with their own children. Insights such as these would not have been possible without using in-depth interviews that allowed for a deeper exploration of the experiences of the coachees.

Observation

"**Observation** involves the systematic viewing, recording, description, analysis and interpretation of people's behaviour in a given setting" (Saunders et al., 2023, p. 390). Observations can be quantitative or qualitative. Here we will consider qualitative observations, often referred to as **participant observation**, where the researcher immerses themselves in the context of those they are studying (Saunders et al., 2023).

Observation. A data collection method that involves systematically watching and recording behaviour, events, or phenomena.

Qualitative observations are usually unstructured and exploratory, but they may become more structured over time as the researcher builds up a theory of what is happening in the situation they are observing (Saunders et al., 2023).

Participant observation. A data collection method where the researcher immerses themselves in the context of the setting or group they are studying.

Using observation as a data collection method involves making several choices regarding how to collect data. These include whether the researcher will join in with whatever the participants are doing (**active observation**) or whether the researcher will be an outside observer (**passive observation**), with varying degrees of participation in the middle of these points. The researcher also needs to decide whether they will tell the participants that they are observing for a piece of research (**overt observation**) or not (**covert observation**) (Rose et al., 2023).

Active observation. A data collection method where the researcher actively takes part in whatever the participants are doing.
Passive observation. A data collection method where the researcher is an outside observer.
Overt observation. A data collection method where participants are aware that they are being observed.
Covert observation. A data collection method where participants are not aware that they are being observed.

Observations are particularly valuable for gaining insights into behaviours or experiences that are not easily verbalised (Perez, 2022) – for example, power dynamics. They also avoid the issue of relying on a participant's memory and interpretation of events, as those events can be observed directly (Rose et al., 2023).

Additionally, they usually have high levels of ecological validity (see Chapter 7), as they occur in natural settings (Saunders et al., 2023). Technology can assist with capturing what is happening during observations – for example, by using video recordings. Videos also allow the observation of something without the researcher actually being present in the situation (Saunders et al., 2023).

How to record the results of observations can be more challenging and usually relies on the researcher keeping a field notebook to keep a record of what is happening and their interpretations of and feelings about that (Rose et al., 2023). Observations are susceptible to certain biases that may reduce the quality of the data that is produced. For example, being unfamiliar or overly familiar with a situation may lead to the researcher misinterpreting what is happening (Saunders et al., 2023). **Observer effects** can also be an issue in observational research, where participants change their behaviour because they know they are being observed (Saunders et al., 2023).

> **Observer effects.** A phenomenon where participants change their behaviour because they are aware they are being observed.

Observation studies are not frequently used in coaching research, despite observations being a good method to gain insights into what is happening in coaching. When they are used, they are more commonly quantitative in nature and involve video recordings of coaching sessions being analysed by trained raters who are tasked with identifying when predefined behaviours occur during a coaching session (e.g., Greif, 2010).

Kauffman and Hodgetts (2016) provide an example of an observation study in coaching. They used a case study of a short coaching intervention to investigate the extent to which a coach's knowledge of various psychological models underpinning coaching (model agility) relates to coaching effectiveness. They focused on four well-known psychological models in coaching: cognitive behavioural, psychoanalytic, positive psychology, and adult development, and they analysed a single coaching session to identify how different psychological lenses may lead to different approaches and different questions used by the coach within a coaching session. They conclude that model agility does support coaching effectiveness.

Observation studies allow us to directly access and analyse what is happening within a coaching session, something that no other methodology permits.

Systematic literature reviews

A **systematic literature review** aims to address the research objective by identifying, critically evaluating, synthesizing, and integrating the findings of relevant research (Cooper, 2003). Researchers conducting a systematic literature review aim to take an unbiased approach to reviewing the literature (Gough et al., 2017). First, they agree inclusion and exclusion criteria to guide their search. These criteria specify which studies they will include and which they will exclude from the final results. Researchers also agree the search terms or key words they will use to search the literature and the databases they will use; these should be as inclusive as possible to capture the largest number of relevant studies. Researchers then systematically search the literature from the specified databases: they use the agreed key terms and apply the inclusion and exclusion criteria, to either keep a study and review it in more detail for their paper or exclude it and ignore the findings. This systematic approach should mean that researchers are not solely including pieces of research that they feel support their arguments and instead take a less biased approach and include all relevant research.

Systematic literature review. A technique used to systematically collect, evaluate, and combine existing research.

Like meta-analyses (see Chapter 7), systematic literature reviews have an important role to play in building our knowledge and understanding of coaching. Systematic literature reviews can be useful to address more open questions, whereas meta-analysis is generally useful to test hypotheses or address more closed questions. Like meta-analyses, the number of systematic literature reviews as well as the specificity of research questions addressed by systematic literature reviews continue to grow in parallel with the number of primary studies in the field of coaching. We will now review three such studies.

In 2018, Bozer and Jones published a systematic literature review which was aimed at addressing the question: What determines coaching effectiveness? In this review, the authors sought to understand the theoretical explanations that are important in explaining coaching effectiveness. They synthesised the findings of 117 empirical studies and identified seven theoretical determinants of coaching that are consistently presented in the coaching literature: self-efficacy, coaching motivation, goal orientation, trust, interpersonal attraction, feedback intervention, and supervisory support.

Pandolfi (2020) conducted a systematic literature review of the active ingredients in coaching with the aim of identifying the **antecedents, mediators**, and moderators through which outcomes are produced in coaching engagements. Pandolfi included 28 articles in her review and in these articles 46 active ingredients were identified. The review found that the existing research tends to focus on coachee and coach characteristics and the coaching relationship as the main active ingredients in effective coaching, with the coaching process and contextual elements remaining largely unexplored areas. She also highlighted neglected aspects of coaching research, such as the need for coaches to be competent in dealing effectively and ethically with all the stakeholders in the tripartite coaching relationship (i.e., between the coach, the coachee, and the organisation).

Antecedents. Variables that predict or influence other variables.
Mediators. Variables that explain relationships between other variables.

Müller and Kotte (2020) conducted a systematic literature review on the occurrence of goal activities in coaching and their association with outcomes. They synthesised findings of 24 empirical studies and identified that previously researched goal activities include goal-setting, goal-setting action and personal development plans, and a goal-focused relationship. Coaches reported that they worked with goals more frequently than coachees. The relationship between goals and outcomes was mixed, with several studies suggesting a positive relationship between goal activities and coaching outcomes, while other studies reporting no relationship. Study design and chosen outcome measures contributed to the contradictory results. Their findings point to possible moderating variables (e.g., coachee characteristics, initiator of goal activity) and potential challenges of involving organisational stakeholders in goal activities. They conclude that the lack of empirical research stands in contrast to the prominent role of goals in the coaching literature.

Systematic literature reviews are an excellent method to enable us to bring together a wide variety of empirical studies and start to make sense of the bigger picture (Oades et al., 2019). We can address open research questions and synthesise findings to theorise what the implications of these combined findings might be for coaching. However, systematic literature reviews can veer towards a more quantitative approach, focusing on variables, relationships, and moderating factors, as observed in some of the studies above. This reflects the dominance of positivistic paradigms in psychology and coaching psychology research. Systematic literature reviews are useful for researchers and students alike though, as they enable the reader to obtain an overview of a whole body of research in one summarised article.

Strengths of qualitative research

Towards the end of Chapter 7 we discussed the strengths and weaknesses of quantitative research. As you might imagine, the strengths and weaknesses of qualitative research are mostly the opposite of those found in quantitative work.

One of the main strengths of qualitative research is its ability to generate a rich and detailed understanding of the lived experience of the participants who take part in the study (Rose et al., 2023). We get to answer questions in coaching that quantitative research cannot, such as "What is the experience of being a coach or a coachee like?". Qualitative data, being associated with the inductive approach, allows us to find out new things that may not be suggested in previous literature. In gathering lots of data from participants in a less structured way, we may identify themes and ideas that have not emerged in previous research. Qualitative work can also be flexible and can adapt to emergent findings as the study progresses (Oades et al., 2019). We can therefore be responsive to the data and explore new insights if and when they emerge.

In coaching, much of what we know about what it means to be a coach or to be coached is based on qualitative research. Even when quantitative research is used, the selection and definition of variables used by quantitative researchers is often derived from existing qualitative studies. Qualitative work is also essential to help us to understand the complexity of what happens within a coaching session and to allow exploration of the highly individualised outcomes that coachees may experience.

Weaknesses of qualitative research

If we approach assessing the quality of qualitative research through the lens of "scientific research", we will always find qualitative work lacking. The flexibility, the high level of researcher involvement, and the lack of standardised procedures mean that qualitative studies are less reliable and less valid than quantitative studies (Oades et al., 2019). The results could differ depending on the point of time at which the data are collected, the particular participants who are involved in the study, or the interpretations of the researchers who conduct the study. A further weakness that applies to qualitative work is that it is often not possible to generalise the results we find outside the sample we collect the data in, as we typically only study a small number of participants and the results are specific to those individuals (Oades et al., 2019).

However, it is argued that qualitative work is not aiming to meet the quality criteria of scientific studies and instead should be judged against quality criteria that are more appropriate to the aims of qualitative research (Saunders et al., 2023). The best known of these qualitative research quality criterion were created by Guba and Lincoln (1981):

- *Credibility.* Do the representations of the participants' data match what the participants intended? Analogous to internal validity.
- *Transferability.* Are sufficient details provided to allow the reader to judge the extent to which the results can be applied outside of the sample? Analogous to external validity and generalisability.
- *Dependability.* Is there a clear record of how the research has evolved throughout the process? Analogous to reliability.
- *Confirmability.* Have steps been taken to ensure interpretations made are based upon the data, and have the influences of the researchers' biases been considered? Analogous to objectivity.

Assessing qualitative work against different quality criteria to quantitative work allows us to appreciate both forms of research in their own right, without needing to compare them to establish which is "better". In practice, however, decision makers may be less inclined to make investments on the basis of qualitative research. When we consider coaching, an HR manager may be less persuaded to buy a costly coaching programme on the basis of detailed analyses of the experiences of 10 coachees on the programme than they are by quantitative research that shows that, on average, 150 coachees on the programme showed statistically significant improvements in goal attainment after completing their coaching.

Further reading and resources

Jones, R. J. (2018, 13 September). How does coaching work? (No. 11, Parts 1 and 2) [Audio podcast episode]. *The Coaching Academic.* Apple Podcasts. https://podcasts.apple.com/gb/podcast/the-coaching-academic-theory-to-practice/id1321572986.

Saunders, M. (2024, 2 September). Mark Saunders on Research Methods. *Qualitative Research Designs and the Research Onion* [Video]. YouTube. https://youtu.be/R7lx90K7X0U?si=4dHY2mnYZhZfy7Az.

Perez, T. (2022). *Ask a Researcher: Teresa Perez on Shadowing, Participant Observation, and Interviews* [Video]. Sage Research Methods. https://doi.org/10.4135/9781529601183.

Qualtrics. (2024). *How to Carry Out Great Interviews in Qualitative Research.* https://www.qualtrics.com/en-gb/experience-management/research/qualitative-research-interview/.

References

Bozer, G., & Jones, R. J. (2018). Understanding the factors that determine workplace coaching effectiveness: A systematic literature review. *European Journal of Work and Organizational Psychology*, *27*(3), 342–361. doi: 10.1080/1359432X.2018.1446946.

Brinkman, S.. & Kvale, S. (2015) *Interviews: Learning the Craft of Qualitative Research Interviewing* (3rd edition). Sage.

Clarke, V., & Braun, V. (2017). Thematic analysis. *The Journal of Positive Psychology*, *12*(3), 297–298.

Cooper, H. (2003). Editorial. *Psychological Bulletin*, *129*(1), 3–9. doi: 10.1037/0033-2909.129.1.3.

Gough, D., Oliver, S., & Thomas, J. (eds). (2017). *An Introduction to Systematic Reviews*. SAGE.

Greif, S. (2010). A new frontier of research and practice: Observation of coaching behaviour. *The Coaching Psychologist*, *6*(2), 97–105.

Guba, E. G., & Lincoln, Y. S. (1981). *Effective Evaluation: Improving the Usefulness of Evaluation Results Through Responsive and Naturalistic Approaches*. Jossey-Bass.

Kauffman, C., & Hodgetts, W. H. (2016). Model agility: Coaching effectiveness and four perspectives on a case study. *Consulting Psychology Journal: Practice and Research*, *68*(2), 157.

Müller, A. A., & Kotte, S. (2020). Of SMART, GROW and goals gone wild: A systematic literature review on the relevance of goal activities in workplace coaching. *International Coaching Psychology Review*, *15*(2), 69–97.

Oades, L., Siokou, C. L., & Slemp, G. (2019). *Coaching and Mentoring Research: A Practical Guide*. SAGE.

Pandolfi, C. (2020). Active ingredients in executive coaching: A systematic literature review. *International Coaching Psychology Review*, *15*(2), 6–30.

Perez, T. (2022). *Ask a Researcher: Teresa Perez on Shadowing, Participant Observation, and Interviews* [Video]. Sage Research Methods. https://doi.org/10.4135/9781529601183.

Quinn, T., Trinh, S. H., & Passmore, J. (2022). An exploration into using LEGO® SERIOUS PLAY® (LSP) within a positive psychology framework in individual coaching: An interpretative phenomenological analysis (IPA). *Coaching: An International Journal of Theory, Research and Practice*, *15*(1), 102–116.

Rose, S., Spinks, N., & Canhoto, A. I. (2023). *Management Research: Applying the Principles of Business Research Methods*. Routledge.

Saunders, M. K., Lewis, P., & Thornhill, A. (2023). *Research Methods for Business Students* (9th edition). Pearson.

Section 4

Key Impacts on Practice

This section in summary:

- Workplace coaching is coaching provided in the workplace by either an internal or external coach but not a leader.
- Coaching offered to all staff is often via digital coaching platforms and is a form of democratising coaching (i.e., increasing access to coaching beyond a privileged few).
- Coaching can accompany key transitions (such as retirement and maternity leave) and provides the coachee with a safe space to explore difficult emotions often associated with the transition.
- When coaching is integrated with development programmes it can help coachees to contextualise learning and explore how to apply learning from the programme to their own working lives.
- Executive coaching provides a confidential sounding board for the most senior executives who may struggle with feelings of isolation and the extreme pressure and responsibility associated with their role.
- Careers are the stories of our working lives.
- Career coaching focuses on supporting coachees to explore and create informed choices, leading to more meaningful employment.

DOI: 10.4324/9781032686448-12

- Career coaching is underpinned by career theory such as career development theory, protean careers, and work identity.
- Career coaching can involve developing clarity on career goals, identifying strengths, exploring identity, action planning, and navigating a successful career transition.
- Career coaching differs from other forms of career support, which tend to be more directive: providing information, education, or advice.
- Coaching in education can include coaching primary and secondary education teachers, coaching primary and secondary education students, and coaching students in higher education.
- Coaching students tends to focus on developing metacognitive skills, which in turn can enhance educational outcomes and student wellbeing.
- Coaching provided to primary and secondary education teachers tends to take a different form to coaching as defined elsewhere in this text, with this coaching being embedded in the job.
- Coaching is distinct from teaching, with educators adopting a coaching role drawing on generic helping skills rather than their subject matter expertise.
- However, the likelihood is that educators navigate through multiple roles, applying coaching or teaching skills depending on the context and the needs of the student.
- Life coaching supports coachees at a holistic level, with coachees often seeking life coaching to address desired improvements in their relationships and day-to-day lives.
- Life coaching evokes coachee awareness around automatic negative thoughts, limiting beliefs, deep fears, or internalised stories or narratives that are impacting their behaviour and fulfilment of life goals.

- Life coaching is commissioned by the individual and is often prompted by reaching a crossroads in life, or by a critical life event such as a milestone birthday, divorce, redundancy, or bereavement.
- Life coaching heavily overlaps with therapy and the practice of life coaching is not free from controversy, with some publicly documented examples of unscrupulous life coaches taking advantage of vulnerable individuals.
- Health coaching is an intervention aimed at enhancing an individual's health and wellbeing by promoting sustainable changes in health-related behaviours.
- A psychological approach frequently utilised by health coaches is motivational interviewing, which is aimed at strengthening the individual's motivation and commitment to their goal by identifying and exploring their reasons for wanting to change.
- Health coaches work with people with physical and/or mental health conditions and those at risk of developing them including coachees experiencing stress, obesity, menopause, mental health challenges, cardiovascular disease, stroke, persistent pain, and end-of-life care.
- Health coaches do not practise medicine, however they do tend to work with coachees over a prolonged period of time and in addition to engaging in traditional coaching functions such as asking open questions and facilitating goal-setting, they may also share information and educational resources.

Chapter 9

Coaching in the Workplace

What is coaching in the workplace?

We define **workplace coaching** as coaching that is provided by an **internal coach** or **external coach** (but not a **line manager**) and that is delivered in the work context, focused primarily on work-based issues. While spillover into other domains such as personal goals is likely, the primary focus of coaching in the workplace is the exploration of work-related goals.

The coaching relationship is distinct from the relationship between line managers and **direct reports**. Leaders can act as coaches, using coaching skills as part of their leadership style, however the dynamics of this coaching interaction differ to coaching when provided by an independent coach. This is because:

> **Workplace coaching.** Coaching provided by an internal or external coach (but not a line manager) that is delivered in the work context and focused primarily on work-based issues.
>
> **Internal coach.** A coach who is employed by the same organisation as the coachee.
>
> **External coach.** A coach who is not employed by the same organisation as the coachee.
>
> **Line manager.** A person in an organisation who is directly responsible for overseeing and managing the work of employees.
>
> **Direct reports.** Employees supervised by a line manager.

DOI: 10.4324/9781032686448-13

- The power balance between line manager and direct report differs to that between coach and coachee. Line managers hold more power than their direct reports, whereas coach and coachee should be level in terms of the power they hold in the relationship
- Line managers need to fulfil a performance management role. A responsibility of a line manager is ensuring their direct reports perform effectively to achieve individual, team, and organisational objectives. This is unlike a coach, who does not hold responsibility for their coachee's progress towards goals (see more on this in Box 9.1 below).
- The nature of the interaction line managers have with direct reports is more varied. Coaching skills might be utilised in more frequent interactions and conversations, as well as more formal one-to-one meetings, whereas coaches will only tend to have formal coaching meetings (whether that is one-to-one, team, or group format) with their coachees

---

Box 9.1   Detachment to coachee progress

One of the greatest challenges in coaching is that coaches should strive to remain detached from the progress of the coachee. This may sound counterintuitive: surely as coaches we want our coachees to make progress towards their goals, as this is likely an indicator of the quality of our coaching? However, as soon as we link our coachee's actions or progress to our own inputs as a coach, it becomes increasingly difficult to maintain a non-judgemental approach and hold unconditional positive regard towards our coachees (as we explored in Chapter 3).

Imagine you are meeting with a coachee for a third coaching session. Your coachee provides an update on their situation over the last month and it becomes clear that the actions they had decided to work on in your last session have not been completed. If, as coach, we hold an attachment to these actions and outcomes, it will be inevitable that we will feel disappointment with our coachee for not making the progress that they wish to make. Even if this disappointment is well meaning (we want the best for them and feel disappointed that things are not improving), it will still impact our connection with our coachee. This will likely hinder the quality of the coaching relationship and consequently the ongoing impact of coaching.

A helpful alternative can be to recognise that everything that happens (or does not happen) is an opportunity to learn. If a coachee finds that they are frequently setting actions and not able to follow through with these, what might that be telling them about themselves, the actions they set, their goals, or their situation? A coach may share the observation of any patterns they notice around lack of progress, and this may prompt an insightful discussion, which could enable the coachee to become more self-aware and ultimately facilitate progress towards action in the future.

Coaches may be either external or internal to the coachee's employing organisation. Internal coaches are employed by the same organisation as the coachee. They may be either full-time (i.e., with the job title of "coach" and coaching forming their primary duties) or they may work as "job plus" coaches, where they still complete the job they were employed by the organisation to perform, but have also been trained in coaching skills and, in addition to their job role, they have a number of internal coachees who they provide coaching for. External coaches are usually self-employed or employed by a coaching organisation.

There is very little research exploring the comparative effectiveness of internal versus external coaches, although Jones and colleagues (2016) were able to test this in their meta-analysis exploring the effectiveness of coaching. They found that while coaching by both internal and external coaches was beneficial for learning and performance, the effect of coaching by internal coaches was stronger compared to that by external coaches. Jones and colleagues (2016) hypothesised that this may be because internal coaches inevitably have a better understanding of the organisation's culture and climate and may therefore be better placed to enable the coachee to be more productive, due to their enhanced understanding of organisation-specific barriers or facilitators to achievement.

What is the underpinning psychology?

The practice of coaching in the workplace draws predominantly on the discipline of **occupational psychology**. Occupational psychology is the field of psychology that applies psychological principles and science to work, businesses, and organisations. Specifically, there are a range of areas of occupational psychology that are relevant to coaching in the workplace, including:

> **Occupational psychology**. The field of psychology that applies psychological principles and science to work, business, and organisations.

- individual differences (such as personality) and attitudes and behaviour at work (such as decision-making)
- motivation
- learning, training and development
- career development
- wellbeing
- leadership
- teams and groups at work
- organisational culture and climate.

It is likely that coaching psychologists who are coaching in the workplace will draw on theory and research from many of the areas listed above in their coaching practice. This could be in relation to the specific interventions they use in a coaching session, such as the use of goal-setting, which is a motivation theory (see Chapter 4 for a detailed discussion of goal-setting in coaching), or supporting their coaching practice by providing an understanding of the underpinning psychology of the issues or challenges their coachee may be facing at work.

Application of coaching in the workplace

There are many different ways in which workplace coaching can be applied in practice. To explore some of these applications in detail, we have grouped them into four types of application. These are:

1 Coaching is offered to all staff.
2 Coaching is offered to support transitions.
3 Coaching is offered in conjunction with development programmes.
4 Coaching is offered to those in executive positions.

Coaching is offered to all staff

It has been cited that only 10 per cent of an organisation's employees will ever enjoy the benefits of being coached (Lyle, 2022). However, many in the coaching profession and beyond do not feel comfortable with the fact that such a small, privileged group are the only people to benefit from coaching. This discomfort around the lack of access to coaching for the majority of people, coupled with the rise of **digital coaching platforms**, means that one-to-one coaching is now being offered at a much broader scale and at a lower cost than ever before.

> **Digital coaching platforms.** Dedicated coaching platforms where everything about the coaching intervention can all happen in the same online place.

Digital coaching platforms are dedicated coaching platforms where everything about the coaching intervention can all happen in the same online place, including:

- assessment of coachees (for example, completion of psychometrics such as personality assessments)
- matching of coachees with coaches
- goal-setting
- session management (i.e., booking and rearranging sessions)
- hosting further learning resources

- delivery of coaching sessions
- evaluation.

Generally, digital coaching platforms utilise coaching provided by external coaches. However, some providers also offer the option for organisations to onboard their internal coaches onto the platform so that the platform can be used for the management of coaching provided by both internal and external coaches.

In response to the opportunities presented by a desire to **democratise** coaching, coupled with improved technological capabilities, a number of digital platform providers (for example,

> **Democratise.** Make something accessible, available, or open to all people.

EZRA, BetterUp, and CoachHub) have made significant gains in the workplace coaching market. These digital coaching platforms enable organisations to bulk-buy coaching "licences" that give large numbers of employees access to unlimited coaching sessions at a competitive price.

This has meant that some organisations are now offering coaching as part of their employee value proposition. The employee value proposition describes the range of benefits that are offered by organisations to employees, to attract prospective employees and retain them once hired (Verlinden, 2024). Offering all employees unlimited coaching sessions sends a very clear signal to employees that they are valued by the organisation and that their development is being prioritised and invested in.

Research by Pillans and colleagues (2023) indicated an intention from organisations to democratise access to coaching. For example, 43 per cent of companies said they are increasing access to external coaches for the wider employee population and 40 per cent said they are increasing access to internal coaches for all employees. However, Pillans and colleagues (2023) reported that few employers have yet to offer unlimited coaching across the board. Instead, they describe how the intention to democratise coaching can mean different approaches in different organisations. For example:

- offering all employees a 45-minute coaching session on any business topic
- making coaching more widely available to specific groups of people, such as all employees above a particular management level
- developing criteria and requiring employees to apply for coaching based on needs that meet the criteria
- using internal coaches to widen access to coaching.

While the principle of democratising coaching has many benefits and utilising coaching for all as part of the employee value proposition can help to position organisations as attractive employers in a competitive job market, offering coaching on a significant scale is not without its disadvantages. Pillans and colleagues (2023) describe how some organisations using digital coaching platforms to offer coaching on a large scale report low adoption rates and wasted costs, as they purchase large numbers of licences for coachees to use the platform that then go unused. In these instances, it would be critical for organisations to explore and understand the reasons why employees are choosing not to engage with the coaching that is being provided. Concerns have also been raised that, while making coaching more affordable is welcome in the pursuit of democratisation, the counterargument is that we need to beware of a "race to the bottom" where quality of coaching and therefore the potential impact and effectiveness of coaching may be compromised (Pillans et al., 2023).

Coaching is offered to support transitions

Pillans and colleagues (2023) suggest that coaching to support transitions is one of the most common applications of coaching, with 13 per cent of organisations in their research stating that they "always" provide coaching to assist with the transition to a more senior role and 72 per cent stating that they "sometimes" do. In addition to supporting the transition to a more senior role, coaching can be offered to support individuals navigating significant life transitions such as retirement or maternity leave.

For many, the transition to retirement can be a stressful life event, with data from large population studies demonstrating that declines in **wellbeing** typically affecting 30 per cent of retirees (Bosse et al., 1991). Interventions to support the retirement process generally focus

Wellbeing. An individual's state of physical, mental, emotional, and social health.

on practical or psychological needs. Most relevant to coaching are the psychological needs of retirees, which can include managing vulnerability due to loss of the work role – something that can prompt a lost sense of self, identity, or purpose.

To investigate the potential impact of coaching to support the transition to retirement, Dodwell (2020) interviewed six UK retirees who had experience of coaching directly prior to retirement. Dodwell found that coaching was used to explore options on "how to retire", such as taking a tapered exit (i.e., gradually reducing their hours and responsibilities). Coaches were valued as sounding boards to clarify decisions to exit and identify the push and pull factors behind the decision on whether to retire. One-to-one coaching pre-retirement was typically employed to support participants through unexpected events like redundancy, which eventually led to early retirement. Such events prompted strong emotional reactions and a lost sense of control. Coaches offered non-judgemental empathy while participants expressed and processed their emotions. Coaching helped participants distinguish what could be controlled from what could not and introduced a forward-facing focus to regain their sense of control. Where participants did not feel in control, pre-retirement coaching offered them an objective, rational, unemotive view of the situation. Coaching techniques that enhanced the coachees' sense of control included planning activities, future-focused goals, and optimism-focused interventions.

Another key life transition that can be supported by coaching is maternity leave and the return to work following it. The process of becoming a mother is a significant transition that can affect women's **identity** and wellbeing

Identity. Qualities, beliefs, experiences, and characteristics that define who a person is.

and can result in a shift in values and priorities. Moffett (2018) explored the impact of maternity coaching by interviewing 11 women who had received maternity coaching. Moffett reported that during coaching some of the main issues that the women focused on related to the practical side of their working arrangements: for example, forming action plans or considering the logistics of juggling childcare and work schedules. However, most notable was the opportunity to discuss and prepare for important conversations that they needed to have, such as with their line manager when preparing for their return to work. The significant role that work held for all the women was reflected in the desire to devote time during coaching sessions to exploring how to raise their profile and plan their return, so that they could ensure they were fully integrated back into the workplace. Coaching content therefore often consisted of preparation and even role-playing these return-to-work conversations. Moffett (2018) reports that the coaching sessions the women received before they returned to work were focused on enabling them to reconnect with their professional identities. Coaches asked probing questions and challenged the women's perceptions of their current situation. This encouraged the coachees to identify priorities, including raising awareness of the women's values and beliefs and how this fitted with their new identity, as both a mother and professional.

The research into the role of coaching to support transitions identifies some consistent themes, regardless of the nature of the transition. This includes providing coachees with a safe space necessary to make sense of the difficult emotions associated with the transition, facilitating a focus on optimism in relation to the transition, providing a sense of control by identifying what can be controlled, and planning actions around these elements, and also by focusing on exploring values, purpose, and identities.

Coaching is offered in conjunction with development programmes

Coaching can be used in partnership with **development programmes**, for example, as part of a leadership development programme or to accelerate the **talent pipeline** for **minoritised groups** such as women or ethnic minority employees. An example of this is women-only leadership development programmes that are employed by organisations to close the gap with the number of women in senior leadership positions.

Development programmes are integral to many organisations' people development strategy. These might be designed and delivered in-house by the organisation's own learning and development team or by an external organisation specialising in leadership development. These development programmes might use one-to-one and/or group coaching in parallel with training sessions and other forms of development such as **360-degree feedback**, mentoring, or **sponsorship** (see Figure 9.1 for an example of leadership development structure), and they usually run over an extended period of many months.

Pillans and colleagues (2023) found that coaching is

Development programmes. Structured initiatives to help individuals learn, grow, acquire and improve new skills, and achieve specific goals.

Talent pipeline. A pool of potential candidates who are being actively nurtured or prepared for current or future roles within an organisation.

Minoritised groups. Communities or groups that experience social, economic, political or cultural exclusion, and disadvantage due to their identity or characteristics.

360-degree feedback. Performance feedback provided by multiple sources, typically including the individual's line manager, direct reports, and peers.

Sponsorship. A professional relationship where a more senior member of staff actively helps advance the career of a more junior member of staff – for example, inviting participation in a high-profile project.

Figure 9.1 Example format of a development programme combining one-to-one and group coaching.

increasingly integrated into development programmes, with 42 per cent of organisations always and 47 per cent sometimes offering coaching as an integral part of development programmes. Pillans and colleagues (2023) also found that 75 per cent of organisations reported that the integration of coaching as part of development programmes was increasing or significantly increasing.

There are a number of benefits to combining coaching with development programmes that are driving organisations towards this application of coaching. For example, attending a leadership development programme is often a time of exploration of identity (for example, "Who am I as a leader?"). Participants can gain a wealth of new knowledge and information shared through training workshops; coaching enables them to digest this information and make sense of it in relation to themselves, enabling them to be more self-aware of their identity as a leader (Bonneywell & Gannon, 2022; Woodruff et al., 2021).

Coaching during a development programme is also an effective tool to assist with exploring how to work on specific recommendations, developing actions to implement when participants return back to their day job (Woodruff et al., 2021). This is particularly important, given that a criticism of traditional training (which still tends to form a substantial component of most development programmes), is that the **transfer of learning** back to the workplace is woefully low (Fitzgerald, 2001). This can often be because learners may find it difficult to understand exactly how to apply generalised information shared in training workshops to their own unique work context (Jones, 2021). Coaching enables coachees to contextualise learning to their own

Transfer of learning. The application of learning, knowledge, skills, or competencies to a work context.

experiences. They can experiment with the coach to understand how to apply their new learning and the coach can support them in creating action plans on how to practise applying the newly acquired knowledge and skills, leading to an increase in learning transfer (Coates, 2013).

However, there are also some considerations for organisations combining coaching with development programmes. It is critical that coachees have a good understanding of what coaching is and how it fits in with the development programme. Coachees can experience dissatisfaction with coaching if it does not meet their expectations. For example, if coachees are expecting their coach to provide advice (such as in mentoring) or to connect them to opportunities in the organisation (such as in sponsorship), they are likely to feel dissatisfied when these functions are not experienced in coaching. Therefore, an important stage in a development programme using coaching is educating participants on what to expect from each of the components of the programme.

Coaching is offered to those in executive positions

Executive coaching describes coaching when it is provided to those holding executive positions in an organisation. Executives are generally those in the most senior leadership

> **Executive coaching.** Coaching provided to coachees who work in very senior leadership positions.

positions in the organisation, such as those individuals occupying the C-suite or at C-level. This describes those top senior executives whose job title tends to start with the letter C (for "chief") such as the chief executive officer (CEO), chief financial officer (CFO), chief operating officer (COO), or chief people officer (CPO). Pillans and colleagues (2023) report that in the organisations they surveyed, the majority stated that executives above a certain level were either sometimes (76 per cent) or always (8 per cent) assigned a coach. Pillans and colleagues (2023) also report that 60 per cent of respondents said external coaching for senior individuals was increasing or significantly increasing.

Fundamentally, there are no major differences between executive coaching and other forms of workplace coaching apart from who the coaching is provided to (i.e., in the case of executive coaching, coaching is provided to someone working in an executive position). However, there are some unique reasons why those working in executive positions might seek or benefit from coaching.

It is often said that "it is lonely at the top" and this saying encapsulates why many executives seek coaching. Elliott (2023) describes how feelings of isolation and loneliness tend to be increasingly common the further up the corporate ladder an individual climbs. This can be because fewer people can relate to the responsibility, pressure, and stress associated with the role. However, even if others could relate to the challenges of an executive role, the hierarchy in the organisation makes it difficult for the most senior executives to share problems with others in the organisation as it can undermine their authority (*The Economist*, 2023). An executive coach can therefore play the role of a trusted confidante to an executive.

Confidentiality rules forbid executives from discussing company problems with random outsiders (*The Economist*, 2023), however executive coaching provides the confidential space where executives can explore the challenges they are facing. Since many executive coaches fulfilled executive roles prior to becoming coaches, they are often able to deeply connect with executives (Berglas, 2002) as they can directly relate and empathise with the challenges the executive is facing. Therefore, the coaching relationship can help to mitigate an executive's feelings of isolation and loneliness (Elliott, 2023). Executives are also likely to receive important challenges to their thinking, reflections, and decisions from coaches that they might not receive elsewhere, given their seniority.

However, there are also some dangers of executive coaching to be considered. For example, executive coaching can be viewed as a status symbol, inflating the sense of self-importance experienced by executives who already hold considerable power in the organisation (*The Economist*, 2023). This is particularly problematic given the high prevalence of **narcissistic** individuals in the most senior roles in the corporate world (Berglas, 2002).

Berglas (2002) also discusses how executive coaches are at their most dangerous when their influence over an

Narcissistic. A personality trait characterised by an excessive pre-occupation with oneself, a need for admiration, and a lack of empathy for others.

executive's decisions becomes too great. This potentially puts the coach in a position to wield great power over an entire organisation – something that may be abused, even if unintentionally. One way in which this risk might be at least partly mitigated is to ensure that coaching interventions, even at the highest level in the organisation, have a finite duration. By avoiding excessively prolonged coaching interventions this might ensure that executives do not form a dependency on their coach.

Box 9.2   Does more expensive equal better?

An interesting aspect of workplace coaching is the huge range of fees being charged by coaches. Coaching is usually charged by the hour and the exact fees coaches charge tend not to be publicly available. Instead, a price is usually provided, upon request, for each coachee or organisation. The price for coaching will either be set by the coach themselves (if they are a self-employed coach) or by their employing organisation (if they work for an organisation that provides coaching services). Coaching provided at scale, often by the digital coaching platforms, may charge in the region of £60 to £100 per session. The average hourly fee charged by coaches is suggested to be $244 (approximately £191) (ICF, 2023). Whereas, executive coaches tend to charge much more, often with huge ranges in prices even between executive coaches. We have even heard of cases where some executive coaches charge as much as $50,000 per session.

A valid assumption might be that the price charged by the coach is linked to the quality or effectiveness of their coaching or even perhaps their level of experience or qualifications, however this generally does not seem to be the case. As we discussed in Chapter 7, effectively quantifying the impact of coaching is complicated, even with a research team at your disposal, therefore it is difficult for executive coaches to concretely make claims about their effectiveness with any level of scientific rigour.

Further reading and resources

Lyle, S. (2022). Why the time is right to democratise coaching. *HR Magazine.* https://www.hrmagazine.co.uk/content/insights/why-the-time-is-right-to-democratise-coaching/.

Rindone, A. (2021). Leaders need professional coaching now more than ever. *Harvard Business Review.* https://hbr.org/sponsored/2021/03/leaders-need-professional-coaching-now-more-than-ever.

The Economist. (2023). Executive coaching is useful therapy that you can expense. Accessed from https://www.economist.com/business/2023/07/13/executive-coaching-is-useful-therapy-that-you-can-expense.

References

Berglas, S. (2002). The very real dangers of executive coaching. *Harvard Business Review.* Accessed from https://hbr.org/2002/06/the-very-real-dangers-of-executive-coaching. Retrieved 1 December 2023.

Bonneywell, S., & Gannon, J. (2022). Maximising female leader development through simultaneous individual and group coaching. *Coaching: An International Journal of Theory, Research and Practice,* 15(2), 180–196.

Bosse, R., Aldwin, C., Levenson, M., and Workman-Daniels, K. (1991). How stressful is retirement? Findings from the Normative Aging Study. *Journal of Gerontology: Psychological Sciences,* 46(1),.9–14. doi: 10.1093/geronj/46.1.P9.

Coates, D. (2013). Integrated leadership development programmes: Are they effective and what role does coaching play? *International Journal of Evidence Based Coaching & Mentoring,* S7, 39–55.

Dodwell, T. (2020). Coaching needs to differ before and after the transition to retirement. *International Journal of Evidence Based Coaching & Mentoring*, *14*, 102–118.

Elliott, K. (2023). Five benefits of executive coaching that might surprise you. *Forbes*. Accessed from https://www.forbes.com/councils/forbescoachescouncil/2023/03/24/five-benefits-of-executive-coaching-that-might-surprise-you/. Retrieved 1 December 2023.

Fitzgerald, R. (2001). The strange case of the transfer of training estimate. *The Industrial-Organizational Psychologist*, *39*(2), 18–19.

ICF (2023). *Global Coaching Study 2023 Executive Summary*. https://coachingfederation.org/app/uploads/2023/04/2023ICFGlobalCoachingStudy_ExecutiveSummary.pdf.

Jones, R. J. (2021). *Coaching with Research in Mind*. Routledge.

Jones, R. J., Woods, S. A., & Guillaume, Y. R. (2016). The effectiveness of workplace coaching: A meta-analysis of learning and performance outcomes from coaching. *Journal of Occupational and Organizational Psychology*, *89*(2), 249–277.

Lyle, S. (2022). Why the time is right to democratise coaching. *HR Magazine*. Accessed from https://www.hrmagazine.co.uk/content/insights/why-the-time-is-right-to-democratise-coaching/. Retrieved 10 November 2023.

Moffett, J. (2018). Adjusting to that new norm: How and why maternity coaching can help with the transition back to work after maternity leave. *International Coaching Psychology Review*, *13*(2), 62–76.

Pillans, G., Jones, R., & Caesar, N. (2023). *Coaching: Maximising Business Impact*. Corporate Research Forum.

The Economist. (2023). Executive coaching is useful therapy that you can expense. Accessed from https://www.economist.com/business/2023/07/13/executive-coaching-is-useful-therapy-that-you-can-expense.

Verlinden, N. (2024). Employee value proposition: All you need to know. Accessed from https://www.aihr.com/blog/employee-value-proposition-evp/. Retrieved 19 January 2024.

Woodruff, T., Lemler, R., & Brown, R. (2021). Lessons for leadership coaching in a leader development intensive environment. *Journal of Character and Leadership Development*, *8*(1), 50–65.

Chapter 10

Career Coaching

What is career coaching?

To understand **career coaching**, we must first understand **"careers"**. Careers can be considered as "the stories of our working lives" (Woods & West, 2019, p. 255). Careers are therefore much more than a series of jobs or even an occupation. We can consider careers in terms of **career development** (i.e., understand different stages in people's careers over the course of their lifespan) and career decision making, which can be linked to the development and influence of **vocational interests**, **strengths**, and **individual differences**.

Career coaching focuses on supporting

Career coaching. Coaching that focuses on supporting coachees in exploring and making informed career choices, leading to more meaningful employment.

Career. A long-term professional journey that involves a series of work-related experiences, roles, and achievements.

Career development. Understanding the different stages in people's careers over the course of their lifespan.

Vocational interests. Preference for certain activities, fields, or types of work.

Strengths. Natural talents, abilities, or qualities that enable an individual to perform well.

Individual differences. Unique characteristics, traits, abilities, and experiences that distinguish one person from another.

DOI: 10.4324/9781032686448-14

coachees to explore and make informed choices, leading to more meaningful employment. The decision to work with a career coach is often motivated by the desire to prepare for an upcoming career decision. For example, a coachee might be seeking a new job or a whole new career path. Alternatively, coachees may have a latent career goal but lack clarity on how to pursue this goal, and so they wish to explore this further with a career coach.

What is the underpinning psychology?

Careers are like stories: each career could be considered to be a work-based autobiography created by an individual through their career aspirations and decisions (Woods & West, 2019). Psychologists are interested in the development of careers over a lifespan and developmental career theories generally identify specific stage of careers. Super's theory (Super & Hall, 1978) can be considered a classic and influential theory in this field. They proposed five career stages, which were set around specific age ranges:

- *Growth*, age 0 to 14 years: Development of career interests, capabilities, and personality traits.
- *Exploration*, age 15 to 24 years: Exploring the world of work; further development of identity and seeking jobs that are consistent with this.
- *Establishment*, age 25 to 44 years: Finds a job or career that matches their identity and interests, seeks to establish themself in this field.
- *Maintenance*, age 45 to 64 years: Seeks to retain the position in the face of new challenges (for example, changes in technology).
- *Decline/disengagement*, age 65+ years: Begins to disengage with work, focusing more on non-work interests prior to retirement.

Despite the influence of Super's career development theory, it has been criticised extensively, including the apparent inflexibility of the theory, which is linked to the ages for each of the stages, and the assumption of a **linear career path**, which is often not the case when career breaks (for example, for childcare) are considered

(Woods & West, 2019). Particularly problematic is the assumption that, once individuals reach the age of 65, they become disengaged with work, consequently supporting prejudiced, ageist views. Therefore, most recognise that Super's theory no longer describes the reality of careers today.

Another prominent perspective to careers is the **boundaryless career** (Arthur & Rousseau, 1996). The boundaryless career is one in which the individual is not constrained to career moves, pathways, or work activities within one employer or organisation. Historically, "a career" was viewed in the context of one organisation. When you joined that organisation, you had a job for life and, therefore, might transition through Super's career stages detailed above in the same organisation. When Arthur and Rousseau introduced their theory of the boundaryless career in the 1990s, a central premise of this theory was interorganisational mobility. Therefore, an individual's career progression was not restricted to one organisation and instead individuals could seek career opportunities in organisations outside their own organisation. Of course, now, this is common practice and in fact it might be seen as unusual for an individual to have worked through their whole career in one single organisation.

The concept of the boundaryless career has been extended beyond interorganisational mobility, to include a decline in the relevance of boundaries imposed by traditional aspirations and markers of career success (i.e., the definition of career "success"). The boundaryless career can be related to and has significant overlap with the concept of the **protean career** (Gubler et al., 2014; Hall, 2002), which explores how career goals might be understood in

Linear career path. Progression in one's career where an individual moves through a series of roles or positions, usually progressing up the hierarchy within the same field or organisation.

Boundaryless career. A career path that is not confined to the traditional linear progression within a single organisation, field, or industry.

the context of broad life goals, whereby an individual seeks to achieve more than the objective markers of success such as salary and status. Therefore, the protean career concept focuses on the individual's motives for following a particular

Protean career. A career path in which individuals take personal responsibility for their own career development and growth, pursuing work that is aligned with their values, interests, and skills.

career path (Gubler et al., 2014). Traditional career success was usually represented by salary increases and hierarchical advancements, often indicated by job title; however, in the protean career concept, Hall and Mirvis (1996) highlight the importance of psychological success, which they define as the sense of pride and accomplishment that comes with knowing that you have achieved your best.

An alternative perspective on career development is the study of work identity. Identity is based on the fundamental assumptions we hold regarding who we are. Selenko and colleagues (2018) present three ways in which work identity might develop through working life:

- *Passively, incrementally:* The experience of work leads to gradual development of identity over time.
- *Actively, incrementally:* People take decisions about careers that align with their identity and values.
- *Actively, transformatively:* People make choices to change their identity and pursue different careers to reflect this.

Understanding the different psychological theories of careers and career development can help coaches explore how to support coachees seeking career coaching. For example, coachees may be wishing to consider their career in relation to:

- their stage in life (Super's career development theory);
- opportunities outside their current organisation (boundaryless career);

- career goals that are important to them and will help them achieve a sense of pride and accomplishment (protean career);
- their identity in the context of their career (work identity).

Box 10.1   A biased perspective to careers?

An important criticism of the psychological study of careers is that, on the whole, career development is considered from an exclusively Western perspective (Woods & West, 2019). Even the notion of a career is based on the aspirations of personal ambition, which features more strongly within Western cultures.

As coaches, it is important that we are aware of our assumptions regarding "careers" and how our own experiences in our own culture might have influenced and shaped this. Awareness of our own assumptions can help to ensure that we can work with our coachees to explore their understanding of their career, free from the influence of our biases.

Application of career coaching

Coachees will often seek the services of a career coach when they are dissatisfied with their current work situation and ready to consider new avenues. They usually have decided that it is the right time to think about alternatives (Yates, 2021). However, career coaching can also be used when a career change is thrust upon them; for example, when facing redundancy or due to ill health or financial or family situations (Yates, 2021).

Career coaching provides coachees with a safe space in which to explore their career ideas and the countless career options they may be faced with, which characterise the complexity of career decisions. An understanding of common career change experiences may prove useful to coaches, allowing for a greater degree of empathy with their coachees, and providing frameworks that may lead coachees to greater insights into their own experiences (Yates et al., 2017). One of the most important goals of career coaching interventions is helping coachees achieve the greatest possible clarity about their career goals and pursuing them with enthusiasm and optimism (Ebner, 2021).

The basic principles and approaches in career coaching are broadly similar to those of workplace coaching; however, career coaches tend to focus their coaching interventions in the following broad categories:

- development of career goals;
- identifying strengths, capabilities, and resources that can be leveraged in a new role/career;
- exploring identity and how this translates for work;
- action planning for the next steps in the career change process;
- navigating a successful transition (see Chapter 9 for a discussion of coaching to support transitions).

Archer and Yates (2017) sought to explore the impact of a four-session coaching programme utilising positive psychology interventions on participants' confidence and career change. To explore this, five mature professional or semi-professional adults who were all considering a career change were interviewed. In session one, coachees' strengths were explored with the aim of building the participants' initial confidence by focusing on what they were good at. To build hope, the second session focused on visualising their best possible future self and identifying steps and resources needed to achieve this. To raise optimism, the third session focused on managing negative thoughts and instead promoting positive thoughts. And the final session focused on building resilience by raising participants' awareness of their existing resources. The coach and participants met every 4 to 6 weeks over a six-month period. One month after the final coaching intervention, the participants were interviewed about their experience of the programme. Results were split into three distinct themes. The first was participants' experience of confidence before coaching, including their experience of negative affect and self-doubt; the second was the participants' experience of confidence during and after the coaching, including an increase in career engagement, increased self-awareness, and optimism for the future. The third focused on what happened in coaching that enabled the change in career confidence, such as developing hope and a shift in ways of thinking. Archer and Yates conclude by suggesting that the development of an optimistic perspective to career change was an indicator of increased confidence and readiness for change, which in turn predicted a greater likelihood that the individual would generate new ideas, take risks, and move forward.

Optimism in the context of career coaching was further explored by Ebner (2021) who investigated a single 90-minute career coaching intervention with 51 university students. Career optimism was defined as expecting the best possible results for one's future career development and being confident with one's career plans (Spurk & Volmer, 2013). Ebner (2021) also examined career insecurity, as she proposed that an important outcome of career coaching is to replace any natural perceptions of career insecurity that would accompany a career transition with a realistic hope for a successful career. Ebner (2021) also examined self-clarity, which is the extent to which an individual's self-image is clearly and convincingly defined, internally consistent and stable (Campbell et al., 1996) and career-goal clarity, which is the extent to which a coachee experiences clarity in relation to their career goals. Ebner (2021) found that during the process of career coaching, there was a significant positive effect of working on coachees' self-clarity and career-goal clarity on their career optimism and career security.

These studies suggest that career coaching brings a sense of clarity and awareness for the coachee in terms of their career which supports a more optimistic, confident, and secure outlook.

Box 10.2   A career coaching technique

An example of a coaching technique that can be particularly helpful in career coaching is Challenge, Action, Result (CAR) (Leach, 2021). This technique can be used to help coachees identify their achievements, which they will need to have clear in their minds, if they are to articulate these during the recruitment process (for example, during an interview). Career coaches can help the coachee to reflect on and consequently identify the achievements that demonstrate their strengths. Some examples of coaching questions for this technique could include:

- *Challenge*: What was the challenge you faced?
- *Action*: What actions did you take to address this challenge?
- *Result*: What was the outcome of the challenge?

How is it different to other types of support?

Career coaching is just one of many forms of career development support, which include support from careers assistants, careers advisers, careers leaders, career counsellors, careers consultants, and career development experts (Career Development Institute, 2024).

The Career Development Institute (2024) outline that career development work can be categorised as careers education, information, advice, and guidance (CEIAG):

- *Careers education*: This usually takes place in education settings. It includes educating people on potential careers available, developing career management skills, and exploring an individual's own career potential.
- *Careers information*: This includes providing information about, for example, different job roles to help people make informed decisions about their career.
- *Careers advice*: Advice is offered on the different career pathways.
- *Careers guidance*: This involves exploring strengths, development opportunities, aspirations, and the need to increase self-awareness to inform career choices. The Career Development Institute position career coaching as a form of career guidance.

What differentiates career coaching and other forms of career development support is that the focus in career coaching is on increasing the coachee's self-awareness in the context of their career choices, with career coaches applying the core principles of coaching explored in Chapter 1 as part of their practice:

- Coaches use questioning and reflecting skills.
- Coaching depends upon a sharing, trusting relationship.
- Coaches avoid giving advice.
- Coaches maintain a belief that people can find their own solutions.
- Coaching is led by the coachee.
- Coaching focuses on the whole person in the context of goal pursuit.

The other forms of career development on the other hand, tend to be more directive, with the career development professional providing information, education, or advice.

Further reading

Jones, A. (2022). Can a career coach find you your dream job? *BBC Worklife*. https://www.bbc.com/worklife/article/20220103-can-a-career-coach-find-you-your-dream-job.

The AC Podcast. (2023). *Discovering the World of Career Coaching*. [Podcast series]. https://www.associationforcoaching.com/page/dl-hub_podcast-channel_career-coaching.

The Coaching Psychology Pod. (2023, 1 August). Coaching careers [Podcast episode]. https://podcasts.apple.com/gb/podcast/coaching-careers/id1608066740?i=1000623019457.

References

Archer, S., & Yates, J. (2017). Understanding potential career changers' experience of career confidence following a positive psychology based coaching programme. *Coaching: An International Journal of Theory, Research and Practice*, 10(2), 157–175.

Arthur, M.B., & Rousseau, D. M. (1996). *The Boundaryless Career: A New Employment Principle for a New Organizational Era*. Oxford University Press.

Campbell, J. D., Trapnell, P. D., Heine, S. J., Katz, I. M., Lavallee, L. F., & Lehman, D. R. (1996). Self-concept clarity: Measurement, personality correlates, and cultural boundaries. *Journal of Personality and Social Psychology*, 70(1), 141–156.

Career Development Institute. (2024). What is career development. Accessed from https://www.thecdi.net/about-us/career-development-and-the-cdi/what-is-career-development. Retrieved 2 February 2024.

Ebner, K. (2021). Promoting career optimism and career security during career coaching: Development and test of a model. *Coaching: An International Journal of Theory, Research and Practice, 14*(1), 20–38.

Gubler, M., Arnold, J., & Coombs, C. (2014). Reassessing the protean career concept: Empirical findings, conceptual components, and measurement. *Journal of Organizational Behavior, 35*(S1), S23–S40.

Hall, D. T. (2002). *Careers In and Out of Organizations.* SAGE.

Hall, D. T., & Mirvis, P. H. (1996). The new protean career. In D. T. Hall & associates (eds), *The Career Is Dead – Long Live the Career: A Relational Approach to Careers* (pp. 15–45). Jossey-Bass.

Leach, C. (2021). Positive psychology coaching for career transition and management. In W.A. Smith, I. Boniwell, & S. Green (eds), *Positive Psychology Coaching in the Workplace.* Springer.

Selenko, E., Berkers, H., Carter, A., Woods, S. A., Otto, K., Urbach, T., & De Witte, H. (2018). On the dynamics of work identity in atypical employment: Setting out a research agenda. *European Journal of Work and Organizational Psychology, 27*(3), 324–334.

Spurk, D., & Volmer, J. (2013). Validierung einer deutschsprachigen Version des Career Futures Inventory (CFI): Berufliche Anpassungsfähigkeit, beruflicher Optimismus, Arbeitsmarktwissen und Berufserfolg [Validation of a German version of the Career Futures Inventory (CFI): Career adaptability, career optimism, job market knowledge, and career success]. *Zeitschrift für Arbeits- und Organisationspsychologie A&O, 57*(2), 77–95.

Super, D. E., & Hall, D. T. (1978). Career development: Exploration and planning. *Annual Review of Psychology, 29*(1), 333–372.

Woods, S. A., & West, M. A. (2019). *The Psychology of Work and Organizations.* Cengage.

Yates, J. (2021). Career coaching. In J. Passmore (ed.), *The Coaches' Handbook. The Complete Practitioner Guide for Professional Coaches.* Routledge.

Yates, J., Oginni, T., Olway, H. & Petzold, T. (2017). Career conversations in coaching: The contribution that career theory can make to coaching practice. *Coaching: An International Journal of Theory, Research and Practice, 10*(1), pp. 82–93. doi: 10.1080/17521882.2017.1287209.

Chapter 11

Coaching in Education

What is it?

Given the focus of coaching on learning, it is perhaps not surprising that there are examples of coaching being adopted throughout all levels of education as a **pedagogical approach**. In addition to being used with students, coaching is also being used with teachers as an approach to support their professional development. Van Nieuwerburgh and Barr (2016) outline a number of ways in which coaching is used in educational settings, including:

> **Pedagogical approach.** The method or strategy used by educators to facilitate learning, particularly focused on children and young adults.

- Coaching to support the professional practice of teachers, often known as instructional coaching.
- Teachers engaging in peer coaching to mutually support their professional practice.
- External coaches working with students to improve their academic performance and other outcomes such as wellbeing.
- Internal coaches working with students to improve outcomes. Internal coaches might include teachers or other students in

DOI: 10.4324/9781032686448-15

either a reciprocal/ **peer coaching** arrangement or a student coaching another student who is it an earlier stage in their studies.

> **Peer coaching.** Coaching provided by someone who is at the same professional level.

Various definitions are offered for **educational coaching**, some of which align relatively closely with the definition of coaching provided in Chapter 1 of this text. Others provide further differentiation between coaching in an educational context compared to other forms of coaching. This is particularly relevant with coaching teachers or **instructional coaching**. For example, Kraft and colleagues (2018) describe the coaching process when coaching teachers as:

> **Educational coaching.** Coaching provided in the context of education, supporting either the practice of educators or the performance and wellbeing of students.
>
> **Instructional coaching.** Coaching provided to teachers to improve their teaching practices.

- *Individualised*: Coaching sessions are one-on-one.
- *Intensive*: Coaches and teachers interact at least every couple of weeks.
- *Sustained*: Teachers receive coaching over an extended period of time.
- *Context specific*: Teachers are coached on their practices within the context of their own classroom.
- *Focused*: Coaches work with teachers to engage in deliberate practice of specific skills.

There are some key differences between the definition of instructional coaching offered by Kraft and colleagues (2018) and the general definitions of coaching. For example, while coaching can occur every couple of weeks, it is not usual practice for all coaching to occur on such an intensive schedule as Kraft and colleagues (2018) describe in an educational context. The context-specific and focused nature of instructional coaching also illustrates that it is a process that is job-embedded, whereas, with other forms of coaching, coaching sessions occur outside of the coachee's normal working environment.

When used in a higher education setting, coaching is defined by the National Academic Advising Association (2017) as a collaborative relationship with a focus on developing self-awareness, building strengths, planning, and clarifying the student's purpose, interests, and values. Jones and Andrews (2019) assert that the ultimate aim of academic coaching of higher education students is to aid the student in the completion of their degree. Conceptualised in this way, coaching in a higher education setting is strongly aligned with the general definition of coaching offered in Chapter 1.

There has been relatively extensive research on the topic of educational coaching, some of which will be explored in this chapter. However, interestingly, despite the evidence supporting the use of coaching in education, coaching has yet to be integrated as a mainstream educational practice across all institutions (McFarlane, 2023).

What is the underpinning psychology?

The purpose of academic coaching is to help students raise their awareness of and understanding of what hinders productive academic behaviours for them. This can be achieved through **self-assessment**, reflection, and goal-setting (Anderson, 2011). Howlett and colleagues (2021) described academic coaching as facilitating a collaborative dialogue between the coach and student, **empowering** the student to:

Self-assessment. The process by which individuals evaluate their own work, behaviours, skills, or learning progress.
Empowering. The process of granting individuals the authority, confidence, or tools to take control.

- Set and work towards achieving their goals.
- Understand their **thinking patterns** and **habits**.

- Understand their strengths and weaknesses.
- Foster self-regulation and effective study skills.

Collectively, these elements can be considered **metacognitive** skills. Weinert (1987) describes metacognition as "second-order cognitions: thoughts about thoughts, knowledge about knowledge, or reflections about actions" (p. 8). Hartman (1998) argues that metacognition is especially important

Habits. Automatic behaviours or routines that individuals engage in regularly, often without conscious thought.

Thinking patterns. Typical ways in which individuals think, process information, and approach problems.

Metacognitive. Awareness and control of one's own thinking process.

Holistic. An approach or perspective that considers the whole rather than simply focusing on individual parts.

because it affects acquisition, comprehension, retention, and application of what is learned. Therefore, academic coaching aims to improve academic achievement, by strengthening metacognitive skills (Howlett et al., 2021) such as self-awareness, self-efficacy, and self-regulation. Academic coaching generally uses a **holistic** approach, which considers how all aspects of the student's environment impact their learning.

This focus on enhancing metacognitive skills may also influence wellbeing. Norman (2020) suggests that where metacognitive activity improves cognitive achievement, such as achieving a higher grade, it may also positively impact wellbeing, as the student experiences positive emotions linked to the cognitive achievement. Norman (2020) also suggests that the metacognitive activity itself may be subjectively experienced as pleasant, which could directly affect a person's current mood and wellbeing. For example, a strong feeling of comprehending a text could be experienced as positive.

In terms of instructional coaching supporting teachers to hone their teaching skills, Pas and colleagues (2022) suggest that coaching impacts teachers by:

- leveraging social interactions to promote modelling;
- encouraging reflection on teaching practices;
- providing the opportunity to map out actions and **implementation intentions**, an important precursor for behavioural change

Reflection on practice and the mapping out of actions are common psychological concepts that occur across most forms of coaching. However, leveraging social interactions to promote **modelling** is relatively unique to instructional coaching and is reflective of the context-specific nature of instructional coaching, as teachers are coached on their practices within the context of their own classroom. The modelling of behaviours in instructional coaching

Implementation intentions. Bridging the gap between intention and action by identifying how, when, and where an action will be achieved.

Modelling. A process in which a person demonstrates desired behaviours.

Observational learning. A type of learning that comes from watching others and imitating their behaviour.

Social learning theory. A psychological theory that explains how people learn from observing others and the influence of the social environment on learning.

is based on the concept of **observational learning**, as outlined by **social learning theory** (Woods & West, 2019). Observational learning suggests that we can learn to behave in a particular way by observing others engaging in the role-modelled behaviour. In the case of instructional coaching, as the coach is based in the classroom with the teacher, there are plentiful opportunities for the coach to role-model behaviours with students for the teacher to observe and then replicate.

Consequently, the underpinning psychology that explains the impact of coaching on outcomes differs based on whether we are considering instructional coaching for teachers or coaching as more traditionally defined but applied to students. Instructional coaching for teachers is a job-embedded intervention that relies on modelling, feedback, and practical application of learning whereas coaching students enhances metacognitive skills, which in turn can improve learning and wellbeing.

When is this used?

In this chapter, we will focus on three examples of coaching in education:

- coaching primary and secondary education teachers;
- coaching primary and secondary education students;
- coaching higher education students.

Coaching primary and secondary education teachers

Research shows that coaching is an effective strategy for ongoing teacher development (e.g., Cornett & Knight, 2009). Although coaching models used when coaching primary and secondary education teachers can vary, many share common elements, such as assessing and prioritising adult and student needs, formulating goal-specific plans, modelling, creating opportunities for practice, and providing ongoing performance feedback to enhance **intervention fidelity** and goal attainment (Kurz et al., 2017). In Switzerland, science education teachers who received individualised content-focused coaching in their own classrooms increased their teaching competency with regard to planning and their students showed higher

Intervention fidelity. The degree to which an intervention is implemented as intended.

learning outcomes compared to a control group (Vogt & Rogalla, 2009). A meta-analysis on the impact of instructional coaching showed a positive impact on student achievement across a sample of 60 studies (Kraft et al., 2018).

Pas and colleagues (2022) examined the impact of coaching teachers using a five-step coaching model:

1 Coaches interviewed teachers to build rapport.
2 Data was collected from the teacher via a checklist survey and three coach-conducted classroom visits.
3 Feedback was provided to the teacher from the coach regarding relative strengths and weaknesses.
4 The teacher and coach participated in collaborative goal-setting.
5 Implementation of actions was discussed, with ongoing monitoring of progress and agreed actions.

Pas and colleagues (2022) found that coaching resulted in changes in teacher practice and student behaviour; the most robust of the findings was for proactive behaviour management on the part of teachers. However, there were no sustained effects by the end of the follow-up year.

Devine and colleagues (2013) found that instructional coaching works best when certain conditions are met: where there is equality of partnership between coach and coachee, where learning and development are supported and led by school leaders, where participation is voluntary, where sufficient time is allowed, where there is quality dialogue and reflective space, and where the coaching is embedded within the school system and closely related to the real-time needs and practices of the teachers in their classrooms. Instructional coaching is an interesting example of how principles from coaching, such as the focus on the relationship and rapport between the coach and the coachee (teacher), a collaborative approach to goal-setting, and focus on actions are combined with other developmental techniques such as observation and providing feedback. The adaption of the application of coaching in instructional coaching means it is difficult to compare the effects of instructional coaching with more traditional applications of coaching as the activities coaches engage in are fundamentally different in both examples. In fact, Quigley

(2023) notes that there is so much variation in instructional coaching that the likely reality is that one school's application of instructional coaching could be wholly different to the application of instructional coaching seen in a school up the road. Kraft and colleagues (2018) also highlight challenges around scaling instructional coaching. For example, most research studies are based on a small sample of participating teachers who have generally volunteered to be coached. If instructional coaching is offered at scale across an institution, this will likely involve providing coaching to teachers who are less interested or do not even want to be coached. Kraft and colleagues (2018) highlight how **buy-in** to instructional coaching is critical; therefore, they recommend that before implementing a school-wide instructional coaching programme, the first step is to ensure that the institution has a culture of regularly providing and receiving constructive feedback.

> **Buy-in.** Gaining acceptance or commitment to a particular plan or initiative.

Coaching primary and secondary education students

Many schools are extending their focus beyond academic performance to recognise their role in supporting the wellbeing of the learner (Waters, 2011). This has an impact on performance and, in response to this recognition, many schools are introducing coaching to support students. A number of research studies have explored the impact of coaching on students within primary and secondary education.

In line with this focus on improving the wellbeing of learners, some studies have utilised wellbeing-related outcomes. For example, with teachers trained in coaching techniques, Green and colleagues (2007) found that, when compared to a control group, coached students experienced improved **coping skills** and **resilience**, increased wellbeing, improved **cognitive hardiness** and **hope**, and decreased levels of **depression**. Following coaching, improvements have also been seen in managing negative thoughts (Green et al., 2013).

In addition to wellbeing-related outcomes, research has also identified positive effects of coaching students on more traditional "performance"-related outcomes. For example, Green and colleagues (2013) found that, when their teachers were trained in cognitive behavioural and solution-focused coaching techniques, Year 11 secondary school students experienced increases in academic **goal-striving**. Similarly, Passmore and Brown (2009) studied newly qualified graduates who were interested in teaching, had no teaching qualifications, but were trained in coaching skills. Over a three-year period, they coached 16-year-old students using a behavioural, goal-focused model, resulting in improved exam performance for the students.

Coping skills. Strategies or techniques to help individuals manage stress and emotions in challenging situations.
Resilience. The ability to recover from challenges and setbacks.
Cognitive hardiness. An individual's ability to perceive and respond to stress in a way that promotes resilience and mental wellbeing.
Hope. A positive emotional state or cognitive process that involves the belief that desired outcomes can be achieved.
Depression. A mental health disorder that is characterised by feelings of hopelessness, sadness, and lack of interest or pleasure in activities.
Goal-striving. Actively working towards and pursuing a goal.

Also in the United Kingdom, Wang (2012) sought to understand how coaching would influence the development of secondary school students' ability to learn and their view of themselves as learners. Students were coached by two teachers and data was collected in the form of classroom observations, **focus groups**, and interviews with students. The findings from students' interviews showed that students experienced an improvement in autonomy and self-awareness of learning identities. Data from the focus groups suggested that coaching enabled students to

Focus groups. A qualitative research method used to gather insights from a small group of people.

feel that they had greater levels of choice in their learning and also that they experienced more personal connections to their enquiry topics. However, students had various responses to coaching relationships and they were becoming more critical about the overall experience of "being coached".

Box 11.1   Do students want to be coached?

Wang's (2012) findings highlights an important point to consider: not all students will respond positively to being coached. Jones and Andrews (2019) argue that, in many cases in the context of higher education, building a coaching relationship between the member of staff and the student, may build a greater personal connection than either party desire. Instead, students may be interested in a far more **transactional** experience dominated by grades and coursework. Despite this, the underlying assumption across almost all the literature on coaching in education reviewed for this chapter is that coaching supports learning and therefore is a positive addition to the classroom, with little or no explicit consideration of how students feel about this addition.

Transactional. Interactions centred around an exchange where each party receives something in return for their participation.

Coaching of higher education students

Academic coaching in higher education emerged as a response to support and improve academic performance among students (Capstick et al., 2019) and there have been a number of research papers that explore the impact of coaching in higher education, with a range of examples of how coaching has been applied, that demonstrate the versatility in how coaching can be used with higher education students.

For example, Saethern and colleagues (2022) conducted an exploratory study within a Norwegian university, where 14 undergraduate students were offered a maximum of seven individual coaching sessions every two weeks, with each session lasting between 45 and 60 minutes. The main findings in this study revealed that, through academic coaching, the participants learned important psychological processes, received emotional support, experienced increased self-regulation, and improved study mastery and implementation ability.

In Israel, 178 undergraduate students who attended traditional lectures plus weekly online health coaching sessions showed significant improvement along several outcome measures related to **goal attainment** and mental well-being when compared with students who only attended traditional lectures (Atad & Grant, 2021). The coaching programme in this study was underpinned by a solution-focused cognitive-behavioural coaching framework. The coaches were 37 second-year MBA students who had attended five half-day workshops to equip them to provide health coaching. In addition, during the time of the study, the health coaches received weekly one-hour group sessions of coaching supervision. Participants in the coaching condition received coaching from their health coaches in a weekly, 40-minute Zoom session. Atad and Grant (2021) found that, compared with students who

Goal attainment. The achievement of a goal.

attended traditional lectures only, students who participated in lectures plus coaching showed greater improvement in goal attainment, resilience, **solution-focused thinking**, and **self-insight**. Indeed, students who did not participate in coaching sessions showed no change in any of these outcome measures over the duration of the course.

> **Solution-focused thinking.** An approach that emphasises finding solutions rather than focusing on problems.
>
> **Self-insight.** The awareness an individual has about themselves.

In addition to the literature such as the two studies described above, which illustrate coaching provided directly to higher education students, McFarlane (2023) was interested in investigating whether providing students with training in coaching skills can help to reduce **burnout** and stress. McFarlane (2023) suggest that while the impact of being coached is well researched, few studies have explored the impact of coach training on an individual coach in their personal and professional life.

> **Burnout.** A state of physical, mental, and emotional exhaustion caused by prolonged stress.

A group of 18 students in year three who had failed to secure an internship pathway were given the option of completing an industry project, undertaking an alternative assignment, or trialling an online coach training initiative (which was credit bearing towards their degree programme). All students selected the coach training. The findings revealed that the programme not only developed professional coaching skills, but also helped students to discover their unique sense of self, develop their empathy, and learn coaching strategies they could use in life and in higher education.

An interesting case example which illustrates the widespread application of coaching in a higher education institute, rather than with isolated instances of cohorts of students, can be found at the Singapore Institute of Technology (SiT). SiT have fully embraced coaching as an effective pedagogical approach, offering a two-day coaching programme to all their teaching staff. Ongoing coaching practice is supported by regular sessions where interested teaching staff come together for further development of their coaching skills and can explore interesting case examples where they have applied coaching with their own students. This widespread adoption of coaching to support teaching and learning has resulted in a range of other coaching activities, such as the development of a coaching-inspired app that aerospace engineering students use to guide their own reflections while on an industry placement and to focus their attention on developing critical professional competencies. It has also inspired a range of coaching in higher education-related research projects and even a textbook focused solely on coaching in higher education (Lim et al., 2024).

An interesting aspect of coaching in higher education is the variety in the types of coaches which have been utilised. Similar to coaching in primary and secondary education, there are examples where coaches are teaching staff who have been equipped with coaching skills. However, there are also examples where independent coaches are utilised (i.e., coaches who do not also teach courses) and where students on other programmes have been trained in coaching skills and coach (often more junior) students – for example, MBA students coaching undergraduate students. As explored in Chapter 1, coaching is an unregulated profession, which means that there is no minimum requirement of training or qualification before an individual can coach someone else. This therefore means that it is not unusual for there to be a great deal of variation in preparation of coaches before they start coaching. This raises some questions. How much training is enough? Do two days of training equip you with sufficient skills to coach another? How might previous skills and experience interact with the requirement for coaching training? For example, do educators who are qualified in teaching in higher education, require fewer days of training in coaching than an MBA student who may be completely new to teaching and learning? If educators are using coaching to support their teaching practice (rather than conducting typical coaching sessions), does this impact the amount of training required?

How is it different to other types of support?

In the context of education, the most obvious intervention to draw comparisons with coaching is teaching. Whitmore (2009) clearly distinguishes between coaching and teaching by stating that coaching is about "helping [people] to learn, rather than teaching them" (p. 10). Jones and Andrews (2019) argue that, although coaching and teaching share a similar objective of fostering the tools, knowledge, and opportunities, the coachees (or students) need to develop themselves, become more effective, and ultimately to learn, the process by which this objective is achieved is very different for coaching and for teaching. Importantly, in most cases, the "coach" is not a subject expert, or at least is not acting in that capacity, and instead is utilising generic helping skills. For example, Lawrence and colleagues (2018) explicitly state that "In the role of coach, faculty are not acting as content experts" (p. 642). Traditionally in the case of coaching, the student takes ownership of the coaching process. Most coaches are trained in supporting students to set their own goals (e.g., Losch et al., 2016), which is in direct contrast to traditional teaching where learning outcomes are set by the teacher/tutor. Wang (2012) notes that when teachers are coaching, they

Co-construction. A collaborative process of building knowledge, understanding, or meaning through a shared interaction.

do significantly less talking and information transmitting in the classroom; instead they generally engage in the **co-construction** of knowledge, and hand responsibility for learning over to the students. Wang (2012) also suggests that, during coaching in an educational context, teachers adopt a mixture of different roles in the coaching relationship: a knowledge expert, a learning coach, a mentor, and a counsellor. Therefore, teachers should be equipped with the ability to respond to the individual learner's need in particular situations, and an ability to make professional judgements regarding which role to take and when in different contexts.

Further reading and resources

Tedx. (2023, 12 April). *Empowering Education: The Essential Role of Coaching. Krizel Rodriguez* [Video]. YouTube. https://www.youtube.com/watch?v=bhu-IyVyP3U.

The Coaching Psychology Pod. (2023, 1 October). *Coaching in Education* (Series 2, Episode 8) [Audio podcast episode]. https://podcasts.apple.com/gb/podcast/coaching-in-education/id1608066 740?i=1000629780768.

The Coaching Psychology Pod. (2023, 1 November). *Coaching in Higher Education* (Series 2, Episode 9) [Audio podcast episode]. https://podcasts.apple.com/gb/podcast/coaching-in-higher-educat ion/id1608066740?i=1000633319557

References

Anderson, L. (2011). A learning resource for developing effective mentorship in practice. *Nursing Standard*, 25(51), 48–56. doi: 10.7748/ns2011.08.25.51.48.c8661.

Atad, O. I., & Grant, A. M. (2021). Evidence-based coaching as a supplement to traditional lectures: Impact on undergraduates' goal attainment and measures of mental well-being. *International Journal of Mentoring and Coaching in Education*, 10(3), 249–266.

Capstick, M. K., Harrell-Williams, L. M., Cockrum, C. D. and West, S. L. (2019). Exploring the effectiveness of academic coaching for academically at-risk college students. *Innovative Higher Education*, 44, 219–231. doi: 10.1007/s10755-019-9459-1.

Cornett, J., & Knight, J. (2009). Research on coaching. In J. Knight (ed.), *Coaching: Approaches and Perspectives* (pp.192–216). Corwin.

Devine, M., Meyers, R., & Houssemand, C. (2013). How can coaching make a positive impact within educational settings? *Procedia – Social and Behavioral Sciences*, 93, 1382–1389.

Green, L. S., Norrish, J. M., Vella-Brodrick, D. A., & Grant, A. M. (2013). Enhancing well-being and goal striving in senior high school students: Comparing evidence-based coaching and positive psychology interventions [Report]. Institute of Coaching, Breaking Research, Scientific Findings from Harnisch Grant Recipients. https://www.the positivityinstitute.com.au/wp-content/uploads/2017/04/Enhanc ing-well-being-and-goal-stiving-in-senior-high-school-students.pdf.

Green, S., Grant, A., & Rynsaardt, J. (2007). Evidence-based life coaching for senior high school students: Building hardiness and hope. *International Coaching Psychology Review*, 2(1), 24–32.

Hartman, H. J. (1998). Metacognition in teaching and learning: An introduction. *Instructional Science*, 26(1), 1–3.

Howlett, M.A., McWilliams, M.A., Rademacher, K., O'Neill, J.C., Maitland, T.L., Abels, K., Demetriou, C., and Panter, A.T. (2021). Investigating the effects of academic coaching on college students' metacognition. *Innovative Higher Education*, 46, 189–204. doi: 10.1007/s10755-020-09533-7.

Jones, R. J., & Andrews, H. (2019). Understanding the rise of faculty–student coaching: An academic capitalism perspective. *Academy of Management Learning & Education*, 18(4), 606–625.

Kraft, M. A., Blazar, D., & Hogan, D. (2018). The effect of teacher coaching on instruction and achievement: A meta-analysis of the causal evidence. *Review of Educational Research*, 88, 547–588. https://doi.org/10.3102/0034654318759268.

Kurz, A., Reddy, L. A., & Glover, T. A. (2017). A multidisciplinary framework of instructional coaching. *Theory Into Practice*, 56(1), 66–77.

Lawrence, E., Dunn, M. W., & Weisfeld-Spolter, S. (2018). Developing leadership potential in graduate students with assessment, self-awareness, reflection and coaching. *Journal of Management Development*, 37(8), 634–651. doi: 10.1108/JMD-11-2017-0390.

Lim, M. S. M., Patel, N. S., & Shahdadpuri, R. (eds). (2024). *Coaching Students in Higher Education: A Solution-Focused Approach to Retention, Performance and Wellbeing.* Taylor & Francis.

Losch, S., Traut-Mattausch, E., Mühlberger, M. D., & Jonas, E. (2016). Comparing the effectiveness of individual coaching, self-coaching, and group training: How leadership makes the difference. *Frontiers in Psychology*, 7, 629. doi: 10.3389/fpsyg.2016.00629.

McFarlane, J. (2023). The impact of a coach training intervention on undergraduate students. *International Journal of Mentoring and Coaching in Education*, 12(3), 284–299.

National Academic Advising Association (2017). Academic Coaching Advising Community. Retrieved from https://nacada.ksu.edu/Resources/Clearinghouse/Academic-Coaching.aspx. Accessed 15 March 2024.

Norman, E. (2020). Why metacognition is not always helpful. *Frontiers in Psychology*, 11, 501599.

Pas, E. T., Borden, L., Debnam, K., De Lucia, D., & Bradshaw, C. P. (2022). Exploring profiles of coaches' fidelity to Double-Check's Motivational Interviewing – embedded coaching: Outcomes associated with fidelity. *Journal of School Psychology*, *92*, 285–298. https://doi.org/10.1016/j.jsp.2022.04.003.

Passmore, J., & Brown, A. (2009). Coaching non-adult students for enhanced examination performance: A longitudinal study. *Coaching: An International Journal of Theory, Research and Practice*, *2*(1), 54–64.

Quigley, A. (2023). Is the "instructional coaching" wave about to crash? *The Confident Teacher*. Accessed from https://www.theconfidentteac her.com/2023/04/is-the-instructional-coaching-wave-about-to-crash//. Retrieved on 17 March 2024.

Saethern, B. B., Glømmen, A. M., Lugo, R., & Ellingsen, P. (2022). Students' experiences of academic coaching in Norway: A pilot study. *International Journal of Mentoring and Coaching in Education*, *11*(4), 349–363.

Van Nieuwerburgh, C., & Barr, M. (2016). Coaching in education. In T. Bachkirova, D. Drake, & G. Spence (eds), *The SAGE Handbook of Coaching* (pp. 505–520). Sage.

Vogt, F., & Rogalla, M. (2009). Developing adaptive teaching competency through coaching. *Teaching and Teacher Education*, *25*, 1051–1060.

Wang, Q. (2012). Coaching for learning: Exploring coaching psychology in enquiry-based learning and development of learning power in secondary education. *Procedia – Social and Behavioral Sciences*, *69*, 177–186.

Waters, L. (2011). A review of school-based positive psychology interventions. *Australian Educational and Developmental Psychologist*, *2*(8), 75–90.

Weinert, F. (1987). Introduction and overview: Metacognition and motivation as determinants of effective learning and understanding. In F. Weinert & R. Kluwe (eds), *Metacognition, Motivation and Understanding* (pp. 1–16). Lawrence Erlbaum.

Whitmore, J. (2009). *Coaching for Performance*. N. Brealey.

Woods, S. A., & West, M. A. (2019). *The Psychology of Work and Organizations*. Cengage.

Chapter 12

Life Coaching

What is it?

Life coaching is the term generally reserved for coaching that is provided for individuals aiming to attain greater fulfilment in life (Cherry, **2024**). Similar to other forms of coaching, the purpose of life coaching is often described as raising the coachees' awareness of what motivates them and what facilitates or hinders action (Ammmentorp et al., 2020).

> **Life coaching.** Coaching aimed at supporting individuals to achieve greater fulfilment in life.

Compared to other forms of coaching previously discussed in this book, such as workplace coaching, career coaching, or coaching in education, life coaching takes a more holistic approach to working with the coachee. Rather than focusing on a narrow aspect of the coachee's life (such as their work, career change, or education), life coaching is positioned as an intervention that can support coachees to work on any aspect of their life (Aboujaoude, 2020). This is not to say that life coaches do not support coachees to explore aspects of their work, career, or education – however, life coaching tends to take a broader view. Often coachees seek life coaching to address desired improvements in their relationships and day-to-day lives (Cherry, 2024).

Aligned with the definition of coaching offered in this book in Chapter 1, life coaching adopts a similar approach. However, a key difference with other forms of coaching is that a life coach is more likely to explore proactively the connections and linkages

DOI: 10.4324/9781032686448-16

between the coachee's different life domains. For example, a workplace coach, even while coaching the whole person, is unlikely to ask specifically about the coachee's personal relationships (for example, with a romantic partner), unless the coachee brings that to the coaching session, whereas romantic relationships would be a legitimate focus of conversation in a life coaching session. Even if the coachee was discussing a work issue, as the remit of the life coach is the whole of the coachee's life, then it is more likely that the impact of work on other aspects of their life would be brought into the coaching conversation.

What is the underpinning psychology?

Life coaching, like many of the other forms of coaching detailed in this book, is underpinned by psychological theories such as person-centred theories, goal-setting theory, and adult learning theory. However, one area of psychology to highlight as being particularly relevant to life coaching is the concept of self-awareness. Carden and colleagues (2022) define self-awareness as an awareness of one's internal state (emotions, cognitions, **physiological responses**), how this drives behaviour (beliefs, values, and motivations), and consequently how this impacts and influences others.

Physiological responses. Automatic changes that occur in the body.

Coaching has been described as providing the space for individuals to reflect on all the components of self-awareness, and "shine a light" on those that need further work (Carden et al., 2022). For example, a study by Ammmentorp and colleagues (2020) that explored the impact of 12 life coaching sessions with 10 young adults with Type 1 diabetes found that the participants obtained better self-awareness, including awareness of how their unconscious thoughts and feelings were able to control their lives, of what motivates them, and of what could lead to desired changes. Self-awareness is so central to coaching that the International Coach Federation (ICF) positions evoking awareness as a core coaching competency. Through coaching, coachees can gain awareness of who they

> **Powerful questions.** Questions that provoke deep thinking, reflection, and insight.

are, what they want, and the obstacles in the way of getting what they want. To facilitate this, coaches use **powerful questions**, sharing careful observations and thoughtful reflections (Powers, 2023).

Increased self-awareness can be particularly helpful for coachees who are dealing with automatic negative thoughts. These are thoughts that pop into our minds involuntarily and not as a product of reflection or reasoning (see Chapter 6 for more on automatic negative thoughts). They are often difficult to switch off and can subsequently impact our behaviour (Neenan & Dryden, 2020). There are many different examples of automative negative thoughts, such as:

- *All-or-nothing thinking*: Seeing events in extreme terms.
- *Magnification/minimisation*: Exaggerating the negative or reducing the positive (or vice versa).
- *Personalisation*: Holding oneself responsible for events one is not responsible for.
- *Emotional reasoning*: An individual believes something is true because they feel strongly about it.
- *Mind-reading*: The assumption by an individual that they know what someone else is thinking even when they have not said what it is.
- *Labelling*: Attaching a general negative label to oneself based on a specific behaviour or experience.
- *Discounting the positive*: Any positive experiences or qualities are disregarded.
- *Shoulds and musts*: Rigid rules imposed on oneself.
- *Fortune-telling*: Believing one can predict the future in consistently accurate ways.

Coaches can help coachees to evoke awareness around these automative negative thoughts, **limiting beliefs**, deep fears, or **internalised narratives** that keep them stuck (Powers, 2023). For example, Ammmentorp and colleagues (2020) describe how participants in their study became aware of "their bigger narrative" through life coaching. They were more aware of their whole-life situation and how different areas of their life influence each other.

Limiting beliefs. Deeply held, often subconscious, thoughts that can hold an individual back from achieving their full potential.

Internalised narratives. Stories or beliefs that people tell themselves about who they are and how they perceive the world them.

Coaching is particularly effective at evoking awareness in order to achieve this awareness. A safe space is needed where people are able to reflect on deeply ingrained negative thoughts, limiting beliefs, fears, or stories without judgement (Carden et al., 2023). Coaches create a **psychologically safe** space through trust in the coaching relationship and by adopting a person centred approach (see Chapter 3), which enables coachees to overcome any **anxiety** and **defensiveness** when they are faced with challenging information or reflections about themselves (Edmonson & Lei, 2014).

Psychologically safe. The belief that one will not be penalised or negatively judged for speaking up, taking risks, and making mistakes.

Anxiety. A natural response to stress characterised by feelings of worry, nervousness, or unease.

Defensiveness. A response where a person reacts to a perceived threat or judgement by protecting themselves, often by denial or justification.

When is this used?

Life coaching is generally funded by the individual, in the same way that the individual might seek therapy or counselling. Therefore, life coaching tends not to be provided by organisations for their employees.[1]

There are a number of factors that influence an individual's decision to seek the services of a life coach. It is not unusual that, when facing a crossroads in life or due to a life event such as a milestone birthday, divorce, redundancy, or bereavement, individuals may engage in **existential** questioning about their life (Miles, 2022), particularly if they feel that they are

Existential. Related to the meaning or purpose of life.

stuck in a rut and their life lacks the enjoyment or purpose they desire. Momentous life occasions can prompt questioning of what the next phase of life holds. Exploring this with a life coach can help an individual to gain the clarity or kickstart that is needed. Miles (2022) suggests that even when the decision to start over has already been made, perhaps with a big change such as a new career or a relocation, the details of that decision might not be fully formed. This is another example of where the services of a life coach might be beneficial, giving people the push and clarity they need to decide what to do next (Bishop, 2024).

As a general aim of life coaching is to support individuals to achieve greater fulfilment in life, when that fulfilment is lacking – for example, when general wellbeing is low – this can prompt someone to seek the services of a life coach. Bishop (2024) describes how the challenging experience of the pandemic meant that in the years since this, people have struggled with their **mental health** and many have been prompted to

Mental health. Psychological and emotional wellbeing.

re-evaluate their life priorities, goals, and values. This has led to a rise in people seeking the services of a life coach. Contributing to this rise is likely the stigma still associated with seeking formal mental health treatment, such as counselling or therapy (Aboujaoude, 2020). Life coaching may be viewed by some as a more socially acceptable version of therapy. Coupled with this, Dieleman and colleagues (2016) suggest that the combination of increasing demand for mental health treatment, frustration with traditional models of mental health treatment, and the shortage of mental health professionals, may also be reasons that are driving individuals to seek life coaching rather than therapy (Aboujaoude, 2020).

Although life coaching tends to take a holistic approach to exploring all aspects of a coachee's life in the pursuit of greater fulfilment, some life coaches also specialise in particular life domains or highlight specific challenges or periods of adversity where life coaching can be beneficial. Cherry (2024) outlines different types of life coaches including:

- dating and relationship coaching
- diet and fitness coaching
- divorce coaching
- family life coaching
- financial coaching
- health and wellness coaching
- addiction and sobriety coaching
- life skills coaching
- mental health coaching
- grief coaching
- spirituality coaching

How is it different to other types of support?

Life coaching closely overlaps with therapy or counselling. Earlier in this chapter, it was argued that some individuals may seek life coaching due to a perceived stigma attached to therapy. Therefore, the reality is that these coachees are also likely to be suitable candidates for therapy.

Cherry (2024) suggests that, while there is overlap between therapy and life coaching, they do have distinct roles and service unique purposes. Cherry (2024) argues that, unlike life coaches, therapists and other mental health professionals focus on healing, treating mental health conditions, and helping people work through trauma and other issues from their past. While working with a life coach may help an individual to deal with certain unresolved issues, life coaches cannot treat mood disorders, anxiety disorders, addiction, or any other mental health condition.

However, this description is problematic for two reasons. First, as outlined in the previous section, addiction and sobriety coaching are specialisms life coaches often report to focus on (Blackbyrn, 2024). Second, a broad-brush dismissal that "any other mental health condition" is the purview of therapy and not coaching does not adequately acknowledge the complexity of the continuum of mental health. Despite the overlap between life coaching and therapy, one clear point of distinction is that life coaches do not provide a diagnosis whereas therapists can (Oprah Daily, 2022). Miles (2022) provides a breakdown of some of the differences between life coaching and therapy. These have been summarised in Table 12.1.

A more critical view is provided by Aboujaoude (2020), who suggests that the distinctions provided by many life coaches between life coaching and therapy hardly separate life coaching from conventional psychotherapy as it is typically practised today. A pertinent point made by Aboujaoude (2020) is that the argument that life coaches work with healthy individuals to increase their capacity and that therapists treat mentally ill individuals, is based on a key assumption. This assumes that life coaches can diagnose mental illness and therefore rule it out or refer elsewhere before deciding to initiate coaching. The basis of this assumption is highly flawed, given that life coaches have had no formal training in diagnosing mental illness.

Table 12.1 Summary of differences between life coaching and therapy (summarised from Miles, 2022)

	Life coaching	*Therapy*
Focus	Life coaches serve as guides through various aspects of an individual's life. They focus on personal growth, achieving goals, behaviour changes, shifting perspectives, and overall self-improvement.	Therapists help an individual to understand their psychological patterns in order to change behaviour. They focus on improving an individual's mental health and emotional wellbeing.
Training and qualifications	Coaching can resemble talking therapy, though coaches are not certified therapists. Life coaches are not required to complete the same training, education, or licensing requirements as therapists.	Therapists are trained mental health professionals. Therapists have education and licence requirements to practice with clients.
Treatment	Life coaching is not mental health treatment or clinical care.	Therapists can diagnose and treat an individual's mental health needs. Some (not all) therapists can prescribe medication for psychological and mental health conditions.

Box 12.1 Controversy and life coaching

Of all of the different types of coaching explored in this text, life coaching is the one that is associated with the most controversy. For example, the potential for fraudulent practices in life coaching has received media attention, as a life coaching "cult" was the subject of a BBC podcast and TV programme (BBC, 2024). The programme outlined the devastating impact imposter "coaches" had on their clients' finances, relationships, and wellbeing.

The opportunity for fraudulent practices is likely due, in part, to the close overlap between life coaching and therapy. When life coaching is targeted at individuals who are tackling periods of adversity in their life, there is the chance that these individuals may be in a more vulnerable position and at risk of being taking advantage of by unscrupulous practitioners positioning themselves as life coaches.

This is particularly concerning given the unregulated nature of the industry and extremely low bar to entry (Bishop, 2022). Although it is possible for life coaches to seek accreditation, such as through the International Coach Federation, as with all coaching, there are no legal requirements for those entering the profession. And, as with all types of coaching, accreditation is not an essential component for practising. With no minimum education requirements and no costs for licensing, entry into the profession of life coaching is extremely easy. Given that life coaches charge between £60 to £160 per hour, Bishop (2024) argues that there are few jobs that promise such high financial reward with such low entry requirements.

Note

1 An exception to this is life coaching in a health context to support general wellness for individuals with health conditions. Life coaching in this context differs to health coaching which is focused on improving physiological outcomes. Health coaching is explored further in Chapter 13.

Further reading and resources

BBC (2023). *A Very British Cult.* BBC Radio 4. [Podcast series]. https://podcasts.apple.com/gb/podcast/a-very-british-cult/id1679737896.

Bishop, K. (2022). *The Seedy Underbelly of the Life Coaching Industry.* https://www.bbc.com/worklife/article/20240206-life-coaching-industry-scams.

Cherry, K. (2024). *What is a Life Coach?* https://www.verywellmind.com/what-is-a-life-coach-4129726.

References

Aboujaoude, E. (2020). Where life coaching ends and therapy begins: Toward a less confusing treatment landscape. *Perspectives on Psychological Science, 15*(4), 973–977. doi: 10.1177/1745691620904962.

Ammmentorp, J., Thomsen, J., Kofoed, P. E., Gregersen, T. A., Bassett, B., & Timmermann, C. (2020). Understanding how different mechanism of life coaching offered to young adults with Type 1 diabetes can improve their ability to see opportunities and overcome barriers. *Patient Education and Counseling, 103*(3), 544–548. doi: 10.1016/j.pec.2019.10.010.

BBC (2024). *A Very British Cult.* Accessed from https://www.bbc.co.uk/programmes/m001krb2. Retrieved 28 March 2024.

Bishop, K. (2022). *The Seedy Underbelly of the Life Coaching Industry.* Accessed from https://www.bbc.com/worklife/article/20240206-life-coaching-industry-scams. Retrieved 28 March 2024.

Bishop 2024: please add – but see query in case the text-ref should have been 2022

Blackbyrn, S. (2024). *The Top Addiction Coaches.* Access from https://coachfoundation.com/blog/top-addiction-coaches/. Retrieved 28 March 2024.

Carden, J., Jones, R. J., & Passmore, J. (2022). Defining self-awareness in the context of adult development: A systematic literature review. *Journal of Management Education, 46*(1), 140–177. doi: 10.1177/1052562921990065.

Carden, J., Jones, R. J., & Passmore, J. (2023). An exploration of the role of coach training in developing self-awareness: A mixed methods study. *Current Psychology, 42*(8), 6164–6178. doi: 10.1007/s12144-021-01929-8.

Cherry, K. (2024). *What is a Life Coach?* Accessed from https://www.verywellmind.com/what-is-a-life-coach-4129726. Retrieved 28 March 2024.

Dieleman, J. L., Baral, R., Birger, M., Bui, A. L., Bulchis, A., Chapin, A., …, Murray, C. J. L. (2016). US spending on personal health care and public health, 1996–2013. *JAMA*, 316, 2627–2646. doi: 10.1001/jama.2016.16885.

Edmonson, A. C., & Lei, Z. (2014). Psychological safety: The history, renaissance, and future of an interpersonal construct. *Annual Review Psychological Organizational Behaviours*, 1(1), 23–43. doi: 10.1146/annurev-orgpsych-031413-091305.

Miles, M. (2022). *What Life Coaching Is (And What It Isn't)*. Accessed from https://www.betterup.com/blog/life-coaching. Retrieved 28 March 2024.

Neenan, M., & Dryden, W. (2020). *Cognitive Behavioural Coaching: A Guide to Problem Solving and Personal Development*. Routledge.

Oprah Daily. (2022). A life coach isn't a therapist, but here's what they do. Accessed from https://www.oprahdaily.com/life/relationships-love/a29465193/what-is-a-life-coach/. Retrieved 28 March 2024.

Powers, J. (2023). *The Powerhouse Guide to ACC, PCC, and MCC Coaching*. Powerhouse Global.

Chapter 13

Health Coaching

What is it?

Health coaching is an intervention aimed at enhancing wellbeing and function by promoting sustainable changes in health-related behaviours (Almeida et al., 2016).

> **Health coaching.** A form of coaching that aims to improve the coachee's health and wellbeing.

It has also been described as an individual education method that can improve health behaviours (Kwon et al., 2024). As with other forms of coaching, in health coaching the focus is on supporting people to self-regulate or be accountable for their own outcomes, in this case, health and wellbeing goals (McGlynn et al., 2022). It is argued that in addition to the benefits of health coaching at the individual coachee-level, health coaching can also reduce costs for the healthcare system as it can improve adherence to healthcare plans, such as lifestyle changes (McGlynn et al., 2022).

Health coaching is conceptualised in various ways. However, there is broad agreement that it is a **patient-centred** approach to goal-setting, learning, and self-regulation that guides, empowers, and motivates an individual to change their behaviour (McGlynn et al., 2022). Health coaching differs from

> **Patient-centred.** An approach to healthcare that prioritises the needs, values, preferences, and unique experiences of the patient.

DOI: 10.4324/9781032686448-17

other forms of coaching described in this text, and the definition of coaching offered in Chapter 1, in that the coach may take a more

> **Directive**. Take control or provide specific instructions or commands.

directive role, leading the change process by providing instruction or education rather than by solely asking questions to create insight and awareness (de Haan & Nilsson, 2023).

The NHS (2023) identify that health coaches support people by:

- focusing on the factors that may be impacting on their health and wellbeing;
- working in partnership to support people in working towards their short- and long-term goals, including making healthier lifestyle choices;
- exploring people's strengths and their understanding of how to use these to manage their health and wellbeing.

Box 13.1   Who are health coaches?

Health coaches work in **non-clinical** roles, providing personalised care. Typically, they will have started their career within the health profession and then trained

> **Non-clinical**. Does not directly involve the provision of medical services; for example, does not involve diagnosis or the prescription of medication.

in health coaching techniques as a secondary skill. Health coaches include dieticians, health education specialists, psychologists, nurses, physiotherapists, occupational therapists, clinical pharmacists, and personal trainers. Health coaches working in the United Kingdom under the NHS are required to have completed a minimum of a four-day accredited health coaching training (NHS, 2023).

What is the underpinning psychology?

One psychological approach frequently adopted in health coaching is **motivational interviewing (MI)**. Anstiss and Passmore (2013) define MI as a collaborative, goal-oriented approach that pays particular attention to the language of change. The aim of MI is to strengthen the individual's motivation and commitment to their goal by identifying and exploring their reasons for wanting to change. Motivational interviewing begins with the assumption of personal autonomy: that people make their own behavioural choices and that their freedom of choice should be honoured (Miller & Rollnick, 2009). Motivational interviewing is often described as **atheoretical**; however, the underpinning principles of MI align with the following psychological theories (Finlay, 2022):

> **Motivational interviewing (MI).** A collaborative, goal-oriented approach that pays particular attention to the language of change.
> **Atheoretical.** An approach or method not based on a specific theory.
> **Transtheoretical model of change.** A psychological framework that helps explain the process and stages of individual change.

- The **transtheoretical model of change** (DiClemente & Velasquez, 1985): this suggests that people who are "ready" for change are more likely to enact it, whereas people who are "not yet ready" may be resistant and avoidant, rejecting any steps towards change.
- Self-determination theory (Deci & Ryan, 2012): this argues that we have an innate psychological need to see our own growth as self-motivated and driven by us rather than as a result of someone else's actions.

Based on these theoretical underpinnings, coaches using MI work through four stages (Miller & Rollnick, 2012):

1 **Engage**: Use empathic and active listening to create an atmosphere in line with the "spirit of MI". MI coaches are encouraged to provide "accurate empathy". Accurate empathy is when the coach does not condone behaviour but reflects back the challenges that the coachee describes in a supportive and nonjudgemental way.
2 **Focus**: Identify the "what". Review the core areas that the coachee wants to work through.
3 **Evoke**: Explore the "why". Establish the coachee's motivation for change and/or, if appropriate, their motivation *not* to change (or their ambivalence towards change). During this stage, a coach can help the coachee by developing discrepancy: that is, the coach supports the coachee in exploring any mismatch between their current actions and their hopes or values.
4 **Plan**: Work on the "how". Support the coachee in stepping towards a change.

As coaching sessions progress, it is likely that coachees may begin to generate **change talk** (Miller & Rollnick, 2012). Change talk is the language people use when they are considering making a behaviour change. Coaches support coachees in exploring and talking about the benefits of making a change. This technique is based on the assumption that by talking positively about change, the coachee is more likely to build their motivation to change and to become aware of how the change is connected to their values, beliefs and goals. Finlay (2022) provides an example of the difference between needs-based change talk such as, "I need to lose weight", compared to commitment-based change talk, "This week I am going to track my calories to make sure that I don't eat more calories than I use".

> **Change talk**. The language used when individuals are considering making a behaviour change.

Finlay (2022) describes how the opposite of change talk is **sustain talk**, where coachees give their reasons for resisting change. This may be by providing counterarguments or stating the reason for not making a change in the first place; for example, "I have lots of social events this weekend so it will be too difficult to stick to my calorie goal". A coach applying MI will explore the **ambivalence** towards change, which can be apparent through the use of sustain talk. For example, coaches might pick up on or reflect back change talk and gently downplay sustain talk, all the while respecting and engaging with the ambivalence that the coachee is expressing. An additional principle in MI is **"rolling with resistance"**, which recognises that confronting someone's resistance to change is not always the most effective technique to help them overcome this resistance. Instead, rolling with resistance might involve the following approaches (Bonham-Carter, 2024):

> **Sustain talk.** The language used when individuals resist making a behaviour change.
> **Ambivalence.** Having mixed or contradictory feelings.
> **Rolling with resistance.** Avoiding direct confrontation if there is resistance.

- Avoid a direct head-on argument.
- Show that you have heard what the other person has said.
- Encourage the other person to come up with possible solutions or alternative behaviours themselves.

Motivational interviewing is one approach that health coaches may call upon. However, given that health coaching is frequently offered over a prolonged period of time and that motivational interviewing is recommended to be used in just one or two sessions (Miller & Rollnick, 2009), it is likely that health coaches will combine MI with other, more generic coaching skills, techniques, and approaches.

Box 13.2   The "right" type of goal?

A key difference in health coaching from many of the other forms of coaching explored in this text is in relation to the goals set by the coachee. A characteristic of all coaching is that the coachee (rather than the coach or some other third party) sets the goal. The freedom for the coachee to set the goal is a critical element of the coachee-led approach to coaching and, from this perspective, there are no right or wrong goals. However, in the context of health coaching, there are clearly some preferred behaviours that normally form the goals set by the coachee; for example, to lose weight, to get fitter, to give up smoking, to drink less, etc. Therefore, the health coach is likely to have a goal in mind when they work with coachees and may even "encourage" the coachee, through questioning, to recognise the "right" type of goal that they should set in the context of their health challenges.

When is this used?

Health coaches work with people with physical and/or mental health conditions and those at risk of developing them (NHS, 2024). Health coaching is relatively well researched and there are a range of studies that describe the impact of health coaching in relation to overcoming a variety of health challenges. This includes: supporting individuals with diabetes (Wolever et al., 2010); coronary heart disease (Vale et al., 2003); menopause (Almeida et al., 2016); obesity/weight management (Hesseldal et al., 2022; Silberman et al., 2020; van Rinsum et al., 2019); liver disease (Kwon et al., 2024); and high blood pressure (Nguyen-Huynh et al., 2022). Significant changes have been observed in coachees in relation to: decreasing depression (Almeida et al., 2016), weight loss (Hesseldal et al., 2022; Kwon et al., 2024; Silberman et al., 2020; van Rinsum et al., 2019); and reductions in blood pressure (Nguyen-Huynh et al., 2022). Health coaching can also be used to support individuals experiencing stress, mental health challenges, cardiovascular disease, stroke, persistent pain, and end of life care (NHS, 2023). Individuals who are referred to health coaching are often characterised by low motivation, complex health and social care needs and issues, and poor experiences of health care services (NHS, 2023).

The role of health coaches is seen as important in supporting positive health outcomes, as patients often ignore the advice of health professionals (Martin et al, 2005). In addition to this, given that the leading causes of death in the UK are attributed to diseases that are not contagious (such as heart disease, cancer, chronic respiratory disease, and diabetes) and approximately 22 per cent of all deaths in the UK are considered avoidable (Office for National Statistics, 2018), health coaches can support patients to make healthy choices in regard to lifestyle behaviours (Thompson, 2019) linked to chronic, not contagious diseases and avoidable deaths (Best, 2021).

Health coaches work in different settings across health and care, including but not limited to primary care, hospitals and secondary care services (NHS, 2023). Health and wellbeing coaches can also support people to stay well while they wait for clinical interventions (e.g., operations; NHS, 2023). Referrals to health coaches can come from a variety of places, such as via **clinical** staff, administrative and managerial staff, charities, or even self-referral. Health coaches can also work with colleagues to target proactively patients who they feel could benefit most from their support. An example of this would be using population health data and/or risk assessment to target people who need support to manage their health and wellbeing or who may be at risk of developing specific health problems (for example, individuals who are identified as being pre-diabetic) (NHS, 2023).

> **Clinical**. Involves the provision of medical services; for example, involves diagnosis or the prescription of medication.

Box 13.3   Supervision

Coaching **supervision** is a formal process facilitating the continuing development of the coach and supporting the

Supervision. Overseeing, guiding, and supporting the work of professionals.

effectiveness of their coaching through reflective practice and sharing of expertise (Association for Coaching, 2024). Coaching supervision serves three functions (Hawkins & Smith, 2006):

1 **Developmental**. Develop the skills, understanding, and capacities of the supervisee.
2 **Resourcing**: Attend to the emotions of the supervisee so that clients' emotions do not negatively impact the coaching practice.
3 **Qualitative**: Ensure the supervisee is providing coaching to the required standard.

Ethical guidance recommends that all coaches, whatever type of coaching they are providing, have regular professional supervision to support ethical

Ethical. Principles and standards that guide behaviour, ensuring that actions are aligned with what is considered morally right and fair.

practice (Lawrence & Whyte, 2014). However, Bachkirova and colleagues (2011) argue that while having a supervisor appears to be essential practice in Europe, this is not a universally held view.

The NHS workforce development framework for health coaches (2023) outlines that supervision is crucial for health coaches. Supervision in health coaching is provided by a person experienced in health coaching and is aimed at supporting the ongoing personal and professional development of the health coach being supervised. Supervision enables health coaches to work through the dynamics and issues of the individual coachees they are supporting, discuss patient-related concerns, and be supported in following appropriate safeguarding procedures (for example, abuse, domestic violence, and support with mental health) (NHS, 2023).

How is it different to other types of support?

Health coaches differ from clinical health professionals who practise medicine and engage in typical tasks, such as reviewing and interpreting laboratory tests and genetic data or making treatment plans based on clinical information (Ashori, 2022). Instead, health coaches focus on supporting individuals to increase their motivation by using behavioural changes focused on activities, rather than by prescribing medication. Other health professionals tend to take a more directive approach, advising patients on the actions they should take, whereas health coaches, while still able to educate and share information with patients, facilitate the patient deciding for themselves what action they should take.

A key difference of health coaching that appears in the coaching literature, compared to many other forms of coaching, is the duration of the intervention. Health coaching is generally applied over a much longer period than other forms of coaching, spanning anywhere between six sessions in total (Nguyen-Huynh et al., 2022) to weekly sessions for six months, then followed by monthly sessions for six months (Hesseldal et al., 2022). This is perhaps not surprising given that the focus of health coaching is to support coachees who are often dealing with long-term health conditions that are unlikely to be improved after a very brief intervention.

Compared to other forms of coaching, the literature illustrates a wider range of applications of health coaching. For example, there are examples of telephone coaching (Nguyen-Huynh et al., 2022), video-call coaching (Silberman et al., 2020), and digital coaching, often provided through an app, with the coach responding

asynchronously to input from the coachee (Hesseldal et al., 2022). The suitability of health coaching to a digital, asynchronous

> **Asynchronously.** Not happening live or in real time.

format is reflected in the type of support provided by health coaches. For example, the role of the coach in providing education (Nguyen-Huynh et al., 2022) is a key feature of health coaching, which is not seen in other forms of coaching. This is illustrated in the research by Van Rinsum and colleagues (2019) who describe that one of the first actions for coaches supporting coachees with weight loss is to provide some basic knowledge about healthy eating choices, such as variation of food, conscious eating, and portion sizes. Health coaches might be more likely to provide coachees with access to further information and resources (Almeida et al., 2016; Nguyen-Huynh et al., 2022) and take a more proactive approach in inspiring them to remain motivated (Hesseldal et al., 2022). This might include providing positive feedback or recommendations on goal attainment and progress (Hesseldal et al., 2022), as well as more traditional coaching functions, such as facilitating goal-setting (Hesseldal et al., 2022; Kwon et al., 2024; Nguyen-Huynh et al, 2022; Silberman et al., 2020) and identifying barriers and facilitators in relation to their goal pursuit (Kwon et al., 2024; Nguyen-Huynh et al., 2022).

Further reading and resources

AC Podcast. (2023, 1 May). The magic of motivational interviewing in coaching (Series 1, Episode 136) [Podcast episode]. https://www.associationforcoaching.com/page/coaching-tools-approaches-podcast-series-motivational-interviewing.

Coaching Psychology Pod. (2023, 1 July). Coaching for health and wellness (Series 2, Episode 5) [Audio podcast episode]. https://podcasts.apple.com/gb/podcast/coaching-for-health-and-wellness/id1608066740?i=1000618946265.

Henley Centre for Coaching. (n.d.). *How Can I Use Motivational Interviewing to Help My Coaching Clients?* Insight Guide #12. https://assets.henley.ac.uk/defaultUploads/18.XOP.102-INSIGHT-TEMPLATE-19-08-18-12-online.pdf.

References

Almeida, O. P., Marsh, K., Murray, K., Hickey, M., Sim, M., Ford, A., & Flicker, L. (2016). Reducing depression during the menopausal transition with health coaching: Results from the healthy menopausal transition randomised controlled trial. *Maturitas, 92*, 41–48.

Anstiss, T., & Passmore, J. (2013). Motivational interviewing approach. In J. Passmore, D. Peterson, & T. Freire (eds). *The Wiley Blackwell Handbook of the Psychology of Coaching and Mentoring.* Wiley.

Ashori, M. (2022). Health coaching vs practicing medicine. Accessed from https://www.digitalnomadphysician.com/health-coaching-vs-practicing-medicine/. Retrieved 27 April 2024.

Association for Coaching. (2024). What is coaching supervision? Access from https://www.associationforcoaching.com/page/WhatisCoachingSupervision. Retrieved 28 April 2024.

Bachkirova, T., Jackson, P., & Clutterbuck, D. (2011). *Coaching and Mentoring Supervision Theory and Practice.* Open University Press; McGraw-Hill.

Best, C. (2021). Health coaching: The role of the practice nurse. Accessed from https://www.practicenursing.com/content/professional/health-coaching-the-role-of-the-practice-nurse/. Retrieved 27 April 2024.

Bonham-Carter, D. (2024). Roll with resistance. Accessed from http://www.davidbonham-carter.com/roll-with-resistance. Retrieved 17 June 2024.

Deci, E. L. & Ryan, R. M. (2012). Self-determination theory in health care and its relations to motivational interviewing: A few comments. *International Journal of Behavioral Nutrition and Physical Activity, 9*(1), 24.

de Haan, E., & Nilsson, V. O. (2023). What can we know about the effectiveness of coaching? A meta-analysis based only on randomized controlled trials. *Academy of Management Learning & Education, 22*(4), 641–661.

DiClemente, C. C. & Velasquez, M. M. (1985) Processes and stages of change: Coping and competence in smoking behavior change. In S. Shiffman & T. A. Willis (eds), *Coping and Substance Abuse.* Academic Press.

Finlay, K. A. (2022). Motivational interviewing coaching: Theory, research and practice. In J. Passmore & S. Leach (eds). *Third Wave Cognitive Behavioural Coaching: Contextual, Behavioural and Neuroscience Approaches for Evidence Based Coaches.* Pavilion Publishing and Media.

Hawkins, P., & Smith, N. (2006). *Coaching, Mentoring and Organizational Consultancy.* Open University Press.

Hesseldal, L., Christensen, J. R., Olesen, T. B., Olsen, M. H., Jakobsen, P. R., Laursen, D. H., ..., & Brandt, C. J. (2022). Long-term weight loss in a primary care-anchored ehealth lifestyle coaching program: Randomized controlled trial. *Journal of Medical Internet Research*, *24*(9), e39741.

Kwon, O. Y., Lee, M. K., Lee, H. W., Kim, H., Lee, J. S., & Jang, Y. (2024). Mobile app-based lifestyle coaching intervention for patients with nonalcoholic fatty liver disease: Randomized controlled trial. *Journal of Medical Internet Research*, *26*, e49839.

Lawrence, P., & Whyte, A. (2014). What is coaching supervision and is it important? *Coaching: An International Journal of Theory, Research and Practice*, *7*(1), 39–55.

Martin, L. R., Williams, S. L., Haskard, K. B., & DiMatteo, M. R. (2005). The challenge of patient adherence. *Therapeutics and Clinical Risk Management*, *1*(3), 189–199.

McGlynn, A., O'Callaghan, C., McDougall, B., Osborne, J., & Harris-Roxas, B. (2022). Translating health coaching training into clinical practice. *International Journal of Environmental Research and Public Health*, *19*(23), 16075.

Miller, W. R., & Rollnick, S. (2009). Ten things that motivational interviewing is not. *Behavioural and Cognitive Psychotherapy*, *37*(2), 129–140.

Miller, W. R., & Rollnick, S. (2012) *Motivational Interviewing: Helping People Change* (3rd edition). Guilford Press.

Nguyen-Huynh, M. N., Young, J. D., Ovbiagele, B., Alexander, J. G., Alexeeff, S., Lee, C., ..., & Sidney, S. (2022). Effect of lifestyle coaching or enhanced pharmacotherapy on blood pressure control among Black adults with persistent uncontrolled hypertension: A cluster randomized clinical trial. *JAMA Network Open*, *5*(5), e2212397–e2212397.

NHS (2023). Workforce development framework for health and well-being coaches. Accessed from https://www.england.nhs.uk/publicat ion/workforce-development-framework-health-and-wellbeing-coac hes/. Retrieved 27 April 2024.

NHS (2024). Health and wellbeing coaches. Accessed from https:// www.england.nhs.uk/personalisedcare/workforce-and-training/hea lth-and-wellbeing-coaches/. Retrieved 27 April 2024.

Office for National Statistics. (2018). Avoidable mortality in the UK. Accessed from https://www.ons.gov.uk/peoplepopulationandco mmunity/healthandsocialcare/causesofdeath/bulletins/avoidabl emortalityinenglandandwales/2018. Retrieved 27 April 2024.

Silberman, J. M., Kaur, M., Sletteland, J., & Venkatesan, A. (2020). Outcomes in a digital weight management intervention with one-on-one health coaching. *PLoS One*, *15*(4), e0232221.

Thompson, S. R. (2019). Supporting patients to make lifestyle choices. *Nursing Standard*, *34*(12), 59–65.

Vale, M. J., Jelinek, M. V., Best, J. D., Dart, A. M., Grigg, L. E., Hare, D. L. ...., & McNeil, J. (2003). Coaching patients on achieving cardiovascular health (COACH): A multicenter randomized trial in patients with coronary heart disease. *Archives of Internal Medicine*, *163*, 2775–2783.

van Rinsum, C., Gerards, S., Rutten, G., Johannesma, M., van de Goor, I., & Kremers, S. (2019). The implementation of the coaching on lifestyle (CooL) intervention: Lessons learnt. *BMC Health Services Research*, *19*, 1–12.

Wolever, R. Q., Dreusicke, M., Fikkan, J., Hawkins, T. V., Yeung, S., Wakefield, J., ..., & Skinner, E. (2010). Integrative health coaching for patients with Type 2 diabetes: A randomized clinical trial. *Diabetes Education*, *36*, 629–639.

Section 5

Key Emerging Areas

This section in summary:

- The quality and quantity of coaching research is increasing as well as the importance placed on coaching research by the professional bodies.
- Chapter 14 focuses on three areas where further research is required: coaching competencies, the impact of coaching in "novel" scenarios, and coach education (including the impact of mentor coaching and indicators of quality coach education).
- Little is known about whether coaching that is aligned with the ICF core competencies makes a difference to coaching outcomes and further research should seek to test this.
- The majority of coaching research is based on homogeneous samples. Future research should seek to understand the effects of coaching across more "novel" scenarios and consequently expand who coaching is offered to.
- Research should explore what content needs to be taught to coaches to enable them to coach effectively. This should include a deeper understanding of how much training is required.
- As coaches become more skilled in utilising technology and digital tools such as digital strengths cards, avatars,

DOI: 10.4324/9781032686448-18

and digital whiteboards, the frequency that these tools will be used in coaching sessions will increase.

- Foundational coaching functions (such as asking open questions to reflect on goals and formulating actions) are likely to be replaced by AI-powered coachbots.
- It is critical that potential bias in the programming of coachbots is addressed.
- Human coaches will need to fill the gap that AI cannot fill, and this is likely to be by taking a systemic approach to explore complex challenges.
- The role of human coaches will be to ask the difficult questions that highlight the role each and every one of us has to play in the big challenges we face, such as climate change and equity, diversity, and inclusion.
- Implications for coaching education will include the requirement for more advanced coach education. This should include developing digital literacy.
- Future developments may support a shift towards greater professionalisation and regulation of the coaching industry.

Chapter 14

Where Do We Go from Here?

Research

Research on the topic of coaching began to increase in volume in the mid-1990s. At this time, we also saw the creation of coaching oriented **journals**, such as the *International Journal of Evidence-Based Coaching and Mentoring* and *Coaching: An International Journal of Theory, Research and Practice*. For many years, coaching research was considered to be atheoretical and generally of poor quality (Briner, 2012); however, the quality in rigour as well as the quantity of coaching research appears to be evolving. A clear indication of this is that these two coaching journals are now listed in the *Chartered Association of Business Schools Academic Journal Guide 2021* (CABS, 2021), which provides ratings of journals to assist researchers in making informed judgements about the outlets they may wish to publish in.

Journals. Academic publications that typically contain articles about research and theory.

There is also an increased focus on coaching research from the professional bodies. For example, the European Mentoring and Coaching Council (EMCC, 2024) outlined in their 2019–2021 strategy that a priority for EMCC was to ensure that research is always in EMCCs DNA, as they position research as key to advancing the professionalisation of the discipline of coaching. Similarly, the British Psychological Society, Division of Coaching Psychology (2024) set a strategic goal to facilitate coaching psychology research. In addition, the International Coach Federation (ICF, 2024a) emphasise that research allows

DOI: 10.4324/9781032686448-19

coaches to work knowledgably and make better decisions in their coaching practice. The ICF outline that they are committed to conducting and curating coaching research to make it easy for their members to access and use. This focus on research from the professional bodies is likely indicative of the belief that "the integrity of any field of practice rests on its intellectual foundations and research, which distinguishes and sustains what works from what is unsubstantiated and fads" (Boyatzis et al., 2022, p. 203).

Despite this growth in coaching research, there are still significant gaps in our knowledge of coaching. In this chapter, we explore our suggestions for where coaching research needs to go next in order to close some of these gaps. We explore three key topics: coaching competencies, impact of coaching in "novel" scenarios, and coach education.

Coaching competencies

Competencies are essential skills that are required to do a job. In the context of coaching, the ICF has developed a set of eight core competencies that they describe as critical for coaches (ICF, 2024b). These core competencies are central to the ICF accreditation process, with ICF accredited coach education programmes needing to teach and assess these core competencies, and with coaches needing to demonstrate the core competencies in a recorded coach session and show their knowledge of the core competencies in a written exam to achieve accreditation (ICF, 2024c). Given that the ICF is the single largest professional body for coaching with almost 50,000 **credentialed** coaches across 143 countries (ICF, 2023a), the emphasis given by the ICF to their core competencies in the education and credential process will likely be having an influence on the types of skills being developed and demonstrated by coaches.

Credentialed. The process of officially recognising or validating a person's qualifications, skills, or expertise in particular field or profession.

However, do we know whether coaching in a way that is aligned with these core competencies makes a difference to coaching outcomes? Boyatzis and colleagues (2022) state that there are no studies of competencies of effective coaches. In the absence of experimental research studies testing the impact of competencies on coaching outcomes, the coaching profession has relied on opinions from subject matter experts and high performers to describe which competencies they believe to be important. However, this approach is problematic given that research in other domains, such as management and leadership, have demonstrated that only around 50 per cent of competencies identified through these descriptive approaches go on to be validated in further research (Boyatzis, 1982).

To take a specific example from the ICF core competencies, competency six is "listens actively". The ICF define this competency as "focuses on what the client is and is not saying to fully understand what is being communicated in the context of the client systems and to support client self-expression" (ICF, 2024b). This competency consists of six "markers" that can be used to assess if the competency is demonstrated. For example, marker two is "reflects or summarises what the client communicated to ensure clarity and understanding" (ICF, 2024b). Therefore, according to the ICF, an indicator of listening actively is the ability to reflect and summarise what the coachee has communicated. While intuitively it makes sense that listening actively is a core competency of coaching, this assumption still needs to be tested empirically. It would be interesting to explore research questions such as:

- What difference does listening actively make compared with other coach competencies? How important is listening actively in relative terms?
- Can a coachee tell whether a coach is listening actively or not and does this make a difference to how they experience the session?
- What indicators are coachees using to decide whether a coach is listening actively or not?
- Are the indicators described by the ICF universally and cross-culturally accepted indicators of listening?

- If a coach displays some but not all of these indicators in a coaching session, does this influence outcomes?

You can see from this initial list of potential research questions that, even taking one of the core competencies, there is so much that we still do not know. A key barrier to conducting this type of research is the complexity of the research design needed. Any research investigating the coaching process, such as the competencies exhibited by the coach, requires recordings of coaching sessions to form a data point in the research and a process for systematically capturing data from these sessions to be created. Despite this complexity, research such as this would be extremely valuable, as not only would it provide us with data on the role of competencies in effective coaching, but also provide us with a scientifically robust method for coding observed coach competencies.

Impact of coaching in "novel" scenarios

In which contexts and for which coachees is coaching effective? Like most psychological research (Henrich et al., 2010), research on coaching has been conducted on relatively **homogeneous** samples that tend to be based in Western countries (predominantly the UK and the USA) made up of White participants (with large proportions of undergraduate and postgraduate students). The lack of diversity in the context of coaching research samples is problematic when we consider that, particularly where quantitative research designs are used, researchers will attempt to draw inferences about coaching in the context of *all* potential coachees. Henrich and colleagues (2010) argue that these assumptions regarding generalisability "underscores the prevalent, though implicit, assumption that the findings derived from a particular sample will generalise broadly; one adult human sample is pretty much the same as the next" (p. 63).

> **Homogeneous.** Something that is uniform or consistent in structure, composition, or character.

This implicit assumption that characterises coaching research and, indeed, coaching practice can be clearly highlighted when we consider gender and racial differences. For example, coaching has been described as a **gender-neutral** activity (O'Neil et al., 2015) and coaching research largely ignores the power dynamics inherent in **racialisation**, including how this shows up in life and organisational contexts (Roche & Passmore, 2023). Peake and Jones (2023) argue that these assumptions highlight the ingrained bias in both the research and practice of coaching which means that the understanding of what influences coaching outcomes, particularly for **marginalised** groups, is severely lacking. These assumptions regarding the generalisability of coaching effectiveness to different samples is even more problematic when we consider that research has demonstrated that coachee personality can influence outcomes from coaching (de Haan et al., 2016; Jones et al., 2014; Jones et al., 2021; Stewart et al., 2008). Therefore, it is likely safe to assume that if personality makes a difference to coaching outcomes, other coachee factors will likely impact the effectiveness of coaching as well.

Gender neutral. Does not distinguish between genders or assume a particular gender identity.

Racialisation. The process by which certain groups of people come to be seen and treated as distinct or different based on their perceived race or ethnicity.

Marginalised. The process by which groups of people are pushed to the periphery of society, where they experience limited access to resource, opportunity, or power.

Coupled with the problematic homogeneity of research samples and implicit assumptions about the generalisability of findings from coaching research, we can also consider the fact that, currently, coaching is not widely available or affordable (Terblanche et al., 2022). Therefore, how might we understand the effects of coaching across more "novel" scenarios and consequently expand who coaching is offered to? Some examples of more novel scenarios that coaching research could explore include:

- coaching marginalised groups, including people of the **global majority** and **neurodiverse** professionals;
- coaching to support challenges that individuals face, including working carers, working parents, and those experiencing the menopause at work;
- coaching in **non-Western** contexts.

Global majority. Racial and ethnic groups that make up most of the world's population. This contrasts with the (often) Western-centric concept of the majority, which is used in many predominantly White societies.

Neurodiverse. Variations in brain function and behaviour, such as autism, ADHD, and dyslexia, are natural differences rather than disorders.

Non-Western. Refers to culture, societies, or perspectives that are not based in or influenced by traditions that originated in Western Europe.

If we can add to the body of evidence that demonstrates that coaching has benefits for different groups of individuals, in different contexts, we can start to build a case for expanding who coaching is offered to in practice. Not only will this benefit those individuals, notwithstanding issues around the cost of coaching, research such as this will start to address the lack of accessibility to coaching and concerns that coaching is reserved for the privileged minority (Inclusive Leadership Company, 2024).

The good news is that research such as this is relatively simple to conduct. Many of the already adopted research designs exploring coaching outcomes can be utilised here, whether they are qualitative studies or quantitative experimental studies (see Chapters 7 and 8), simply accessing unique populations such as some of those suggested above. An additional requirement here is that researchers take a detailed approach in describing the characteristics of their research sample, which will enable us to begin to challenge the assumptions that findings from homogeneous research samples can be generalised.

Coach education

Coaching is big business. The industry is said to generate $4.564 billion globally with an estimated 109,200 certified coach practitioners worldwide (ICF, 2023b). And, if coaching is big business, so too is coach education. Despite this, there is virtually no research on how to educate coaches effectively and very few coach training programmes are underpinned by scientific evidence (Carden et al., 2023). Therefore, our final suggestion for the future of coaching research is centred on the theme of coach education. In this section we explore two specific aspects of coach education: the impact of **mentor coaching** and indicators of coach education quality.

Mentor coaching. Providing professional support in achieving and demonstrating the levels of coaching competency as required by the desired credential level.

Impact of mentor coaching

Mentor coaching is an aspect of coach development that is unique to the ICF. However, given that the ICF is the single largest coach accreditor (ICF, 2023a), we suggest that understanding the impact of mentor coaching is an important area for research to explore.

The purpose of mentor coaching is to provide professional assistance to coaches to enable them to demonstrate the levels of coaching competency required in the ICF credential process, and therefore closely tied to working with the ICF coach competencies (Passmore & Sinclair, 2020). Mentor coaches provide a combination of coaching, mentoring, and feedback based on the observation of recorded coaching sessions to increase the coach's awareness of their strengths and areas of development in alignment with the ICF core competencies. A broad goal of mentor coaching, in addition to supporting the ongoing professional development of the coach, is to enable the coach to identify a suitable recording to submit to the ICF as part of the accreditation process.

Passmore and Sinclair (2020) describe that mentor coaching should take place over an extended time (the ICF require a minimum period of three months), with the mentor coaching being highly focused on the core coaching competencies rather than any other aspects of coaching practice (e.g., building their coaching business, work-life balance, ethical dilemmas, etc.). For accreditation purposes, the ICF require that the coach has completed ten hours of mentor coaching which can include solely one-to-one sessions or a combination of one-to-one and group sessions. Mentor coaching can be designed and delivered in many different ways, however sessions tend to involve:

- discussion of and feedback on recordings of coaching;
- coaches coaching each other in live group sessions;
- the coach coaching the mentor;
- group discussion of the coaching competencies with case examples.

Our initial literature search in preparation for this chapter did not identify any research papers on mentor coaching. This may be linked to the fact that, currently, mentor coaching is a requirement for accreditation through the ICF only, and therefore mentor coaching is not universal. However, our first-hand experience of mentor coaching is that it can be extremely impactful and, anecdotally, there are certain elements of mentor coaching that appear to be more impactful than others. However, would these anecdotal experiences be supported by the research evidence? Some potential research questions to explore mentor coaching might include:

- What is the impact of mentor coaching on developing coaching competencies and coaching effectiveness?
- What are the most impactful exercises in mentor coaching? How can mentor coaching be structured to maximise the impact?
- What are the benefits of one-to-one mentor coaching versus group mentor coaching?

Exploring mentor coaching through research is particularly relevant as mentor coaching is often integrated into coach education when the qualification programme is accredited by the ICF. If research evidence supports the use of mentor coaching and can provide further direction on the design of mentor coaching, this will help to improve processes in educating coaches. Likewise, if research evidence cannot support the use of this approach in developing coaches, it can enable coach educators to make informed choices about what to include or exclude in the design of their programme.

Part of the challenge with conducting research to explore the impact of mentor coaching is the potential complexity of the research designs. For example, multiple experimental conditions are likely to be required (for example, mentor coaching condition and no mentor coaching condition, conditions using different mentor coaching exercises, or one-to-one versus group mentor coaching). A methodology to collect coach performance data as measured against the coaching competencies would need to be developed and outcome data collected from coachees at multiple time points. A research design such as this is not impossible, but it can be challenging, time consuming, and labour intensive to recruit the required number of participants and collect the multiple types of data needed across multiple time points.

Indicators of quality coach education

What are the indicators that can be used to establish coach and coach education quality? As coaching is still an unregulated profession, there are no universally agreed indicators that can be used. Accreditation is one route, however, that is not without problems. The process by which accrediting bodies award accreditation varies and often relies on a self-declaration of hours of coaching logged, with no way of proving that this is accurate. The question of number of hours logged as an indicator of coach quality is also problematic: how do we know that the coaching provided was "good" coaching? It is perfectly possible that many hours of poor coaching could be accrued and submitted as evidence of quality coaching in an accreditation process.

An alternative indicator is to consider the nature of education and training the coach received. However, this also can vary widely, with some coaches never receiving any direct coach training (for example, qualified occupational psychologists may assume that their psychological training equips them to provide coaching without pursuing a separate coaching qualification). Courses can also vary from as little as a day or two to multiple years in the case of **Master's-level** or **doctoral-level** qualifications.

Master's level. An advanced academic level of study beyond the undergraduate bachelor's degree. **Doctoral level**. The highest level of academic study.

In addition to the length of study, little is known about what should be taught about coaching to equip individuals to be effective coaches. For example, the core skills of coaching (e.g., listening and asking questions) tend to be present in all coaching courses. But what of some of the other elements that are important, such as the areas covered in this text? How much theory is needed to be an effective coach? For example, can coaches learn a questioning technique to help coachees to form goals, or do they also need to understand the underlying theory in goal-setting to be effective coaches? Certainly, we could argue that this would help coaches to understand why it is important for their coachees to articulate goals. How about ethical considerations? What education is necessary to equip coaches with the resources needed to handle complex ethical issues, such as when the topic explored in coaching moves beyond their range of competence or when the needs of the individual coachee and the **sponsor organisation** do not align? There is also the question of how much education is necessary on the core coaching competencies versus the **tools and techniques**

Sponsor organisation. The organisation responsible for financing a specific programme or activity. **Tools and techniques**. Frameworks and exercises used by coaches within the coaching session.

that can be used in coaching practice (such as the GROW model, motivational interviewing, and constellations). Do coaches need these tools and techniques to be effective coaches? How much education is necessary to equip coaches to be able to use a coaching tool or technique effectively? Finally, how do we "teach" coaches to adopt unconditional positive regard, a **non-judgemental attitude**, **openness**, and curiosity with their coachees?

Non-judgemental attitude. The practice of accepting others without criticism, bias, or preconceived opinions.

Openness. A psychological trait that indicates a willingness to engage with new experiences, ideas, and perspectives.

Future research could seek to delve deeper into understanding what it takes to educate coaches effectively, which in turn could form indicators of coach education quality. Qualitative research could explore, with coaches, what it was about their coach education experience that they perceive to be the most impactful and why, to allow us first to identify which components seem to be the most important, especially in hindsight, now that coaches are working and using their coaching skills regularly, and second, why they feel this was important. Quantitative research designs could seek to compare different coach education conditions, emphasising different content or utilising different teaching methods, and track coaching effectiveness outcomes post-coach education. This would enable us to start to build a picture with regard to how to educate coaches in a way that maximises coaching impact.

Further reading and resources

AC Podcast. (2022, 31 January). Research evidence-based AI coaching (071) [Podcast episode]. https://www.associationforcoaching.com/page/dl-hub_podcast-channel_tic_research-evidence-based-ai-coaching.

AC Podcast. (2024). *Research in Coaching: Sparking Inquiry, Cultivating Practice* [Podcast series]. https://www.associationforcoaching.com/page/dl-hub_podcast-channel_research-coaching.

Institute of Coaching. (2022, 29 April). *The Grand Challenge for the Future of Coaching: Richard Boyatzis* [Video]. YouTube. https://www.youtube.com/watch?v=rcQkoPBBmVI.

References

Boyatzis, R. E. (1982). *The Competent Manager: A Model for Effective Performance*. Wiley.

Boyatzis, R. E., Hullinger, A., Ehasz, S. F., Harvey, J., Tassarotti, S., Gallotti, A., & Penafort, F. (2022). The grand challenge for research on the future of coaching. *The Journal of Applied Behavioral Science*, *58*(2), 202–222.

Briner, R. (2012). Does coaching work and does anyone really care? *OP Matters*, *16*(17), 4–12.

British Psychological Society (2024). Division of coaching psychology. Accessed from https://www.bps.org.uk/member-networks/division-coaching-psychology. Retrieved 2nd June 2024.

CABS (2021). *Academic Journal Guide 2021*. Accessed from https://charteredabs.org/academic-journal-guide/academic-journal-guide-2021. Retrieved 17 June 2024.

Carden, J., Jones, R. J., & Passmore, J. (2023). An exploration of the role of coach training in developing self-awareness: A mixed methods study. *Current Psychology*, *42*(8), 6164–6178.

de Haan, E., Grant, A. M., Burger, Y., & Eriksson, P. O. (2016). A large-scale study of executive and workplace coaching: The relative contributions of relationship, personality match, and self-efficacy. *Consulting Psychology Journal: Practice and Research*, *68*(3), 189–207. https://doi.org/10.1037/cpb0000058.

EMCC (2024). Research. Access from https://www.emccglobal.org/research/. Retrieved 2 June 2024.

Henrich, J., Heine, S. J., & Norenzayan, A. (2010). The weirdest people in the world? *Behavioral and Brain Sciences*, *33*(2–3), 61–83.

ICF (2023a). Professional coaches membership and credentialling fact sheet. Accessed from https://coachingfederation.org/app/uploads/2023/02/February2023_FactSheet.pdf. Retrieved 3 June 2024.

ICF (2023b). Global coaching study 2023 Executive summary. https://coachingfederation.org/app/uploads/2023/04/2023ICFGlobalCoachingStudy_ExecutiveSummary.pdf.

ICF (2024a). It's not always what you know, but when you know it. Accessed from https://coachingfederation.org/research. Retrieved 2 June 2024.

ICF (2024b). ICF core competencies. Accessed from https://coachingfederation.org/credentials-and-standards/core-competencies. Retrieved 3 June 2024.

ICF (2024c). How to apply for an ICF credential. Accessed from https://coachingfederation.org/credentials-and-standards/how-to-apply. Retrieved 3 June 2024.

Inclusive Leadership Company (2024). Coaching and ED&I: Implications and opportunities. Accessed from https://inclusiveleadershipcompany.com/coaching-and-edi-implications-and-opportunities/. Retrieved 4 June 2024.

Jones, R. J., Woods, S. A., & Hutchinson, E. (2014). The influence of the Five Factor Model of personality on the perceived effectiveness of executive coaching. *International Journal of Evidence Based Coaching and Mentoring*, *12*(2), 109–118. https://doi.org/10.1111/j.1744-6570.2003.tb00152.x.

Jones, R. J., Woods, S. A., & Zhou, Y. (2021). The effects of coachee personality and goal orientation on performance improvement following coaching: A controlled field experiment. *Applied Psychology*, *70*(2), 420–458.

O'Neil, D. A., Hopkins, M. M., & Bilimoria, D. (2015). A framework for developing women leaders: Applications to executive coaching. *The Journal of Applied Behavioral Science*, *51*(2), 253–276.

Passmore, J., & Sinclair, T. (2020). *Becoming a Coach: The Essential ICF Guide*. Springer Nature.

Peake, S., & Jones, R. J. (2023). The power of group coaching for women. Accessed from https://shapetalent.com/wp-content/uploads/2023/11/Shape-Talent-Group-Coaching-for-Women-White-paper.pdf. Retrieved 4 June 2024.

Roche, C., & Passmore, J. (2023). Anti-racism in coaching: A global call to action. *Coaching: An International Journal of Theory, Research and Practice*, *16*(1), 115–132.

Stewart, L. J., Palmer, S., Wilkin, H., & Kerrin, M. (2008). The influence of character: Does personality impact coaching success? *International Journal of Evidence Based Coaching and Mentoring*, *6*(1), 32–42.

Terblanche, N., Molyn, J., De Haan, E., & Nilsson, V. O. (2022). Coaching at scale: investigating the efficacy of artificial intelligence coaching. *International Journal of Evidence Based Coaching & Mentoring*, *20*(2), 20–36.

Chapter 15

Where Do We Go from Here?

Practice

There is no denying that the coaching industry continues to grow. It is reported that since 2019, the coaching industry has grown 62 per cent with an estimated 109,200 coaches worldwide, a 54 per cent increase since 2019 (ICF, 2023). Projections are that by 2032, online coaching is expected to be an $11.7 billion global market compared to current estimates of a $4.564 billion global market (ICF, 2023). If these predictions are accurate, then the consensus is that coaching is here to stay. However, what can we expect from the future of coaching practice? In this chapter, we explore our predictions for the future of coaching practice and focus on three key areas: the use of **digital coaching tools**, the application of **artificial intelligence (AI)** to coaching, and systemic coaching including **climate conscious coaching** and equity, diversity, and inclusion (EDI) in coaching.

Digital coaching tools. Software platforms and applications that are designed to support coaches to deliver coaching remotely.

Artificial intelligence (AI). Simulation of human intelligence by machines.

Climate conscious coaching. A growing movement in coaching that raises awareness of and responsibility for climate change and sustainability issues.

DOI: 10.4324/9781032686448-20

Technology and coaching

Like many professions and industries, coaching is in the middle of a technological revolution, therefore an essential topic for a chapter on the future of coaching practice is technology. In this section, we explore two separate elements of technology and coaching: digital tools and AI.

Digital tools and coaching

Digital tools can be broadly described as programs, websites, applications, and other internet and computerised resources that can be used to facilitate, enhance, and execute the work that we do (Digital Tools, 2024). Therefore, when we consider how digital tools might be used to support the practice of coaching, we can consider a broad range of resources. Perhaps the biggest shift in coaching in the context of digital tools is the rise of online coaching, using video conferencing platforms such as Microsoft Teams and Zoom. In fact, most coaching is now provided online (Passmore & Tee, 2023), with this shift from face-to-face coaching happening virtually overnight in response to social distancing restrictions imposed during the COVID-19 pandemic.

In addition to using video conferencing platforms to coach online, coaches may also utilise a range of digital tools to either support the administration of their coaching practice, such as email, invoicing software, and diary scheduling apps, or digital tools that can be used in a coaching session. We predict that the biggest shift in the future practice of coaching is that we will see a greater integration of digital tools within online coaching sessions. Many digital tools already exist; however, our experience is that, so far, there has not been widespread adoption of such tools. As coaches become more skilled in utilising technology and digital tools, the frequency with which these tools will be used in coaching sessions will increase. They will likely include:

- automatic transcription of coaching sessions and use of these transcripts for note taking and sharing with the coachee for further reflection;

- use of avatars for role-play exercises.
- digital **strengths cards**;
- digital **Lego Serious Play**;
- digital whiteboards for use in techniques such as constellations.

Strengths cards. A development tool to help individuals identify, reflect on, and explore their strengths.

Lego Serious Play. A development tool using Lego bricks to help individuals to think more deeply, reflect, and express ideas.

AI and coaching

AI technologies have the potential to enhance efficiency and productivity, consequently revolutionising how people work (Li & Kim, 2024). AI refers to machines performing the cognitive functions typically associated with humans, including learning, interacting, problem solving, and displaying creativity. In their 2021 paper, Graßmann and Schermuly define AI coaching as a machine-assisted, systematic process to help coachees set professional goals and construct solutions to achieve them efficiently. AI continues to learn based on data collected from its interactions. Therefore, AI coaching can use the data gathered in the moment, to learn how to be more effective, such as by being able to make the best selection of tools and exercises or questions to ask. Therefore, AI cannot only learn from one coaching process to the next, but it can also adapt itself even while working with the same coachee.

AI coaching can come in many shapes and forms. This includes one extreme where human coaches are fully replaced by AI with what are commonly called **coachbots**. These AI powered coachbots can coach humans using **algorithms**, often

Coachbot. An AI-powered digital tool or platform designed to replicate coaching.

Algorithm. Step-by-step procedure or formula that a computer or person follows to achieve a particular goal.

based on and shaped by large data sets they collect over time, to respond to inputs from the coachee with coaching questions and to prompt goal-setting and reflection. The other extreme is where human coaches use AI to support their practice. This can include using software to record and analyse coaching sessions to assist coaches with improving their practice with AI-assisted insights (such as summaries on the amount of time the coach was talking, the percentage of closed versus open questions, etc.).

When we consider the use of coachbots, it is argued that there are several benefits for coachees, such as the perceived lack of **bias** from an AI coachbot compared to a human (Mai et al., 2022), increased cost efficiency, and flexibility (Diller, 2024). In addition, there is a general consensus across the literature and practice alike that, while coach-

Bias. A tendency to favour a particular perspective, belief, or group, often in a way that is unfair or uninformed.

bots cannot replicate all aspects of coaching provided by a human coach, they are helpful for certain coaching aspects, such as asking questions to facilitate reflection on strengths and approaches as well as guiding coachees through decision-making processes (Graßmann and Schermuly 2021). Graßmann and Schermuly (2021) explore how AI might be deployed in coaching from a theoretical perspective. They suggest that AI coaching encounters the greatest difficulties with coachees' problem identification and argue that while AI can ask questions to initiate coachees' to reflect on what may be the core problem, currently, as AI coachbots do not actually think, but rather imitate and create the illusion of an intelligent conversation, they cannot understand the coachees' intention and therefore explore what a coachees' core problem could be. There are too many options that are ill-defined and, even if it were possible, AI would demand large data sets for every option to create the appropriate algorithm to set a response for each option. AI coaching may therefore only work well if the coachee is already aware of the core problem and simply needs to be prompted with questions to reflect upon it. Likewise, because AI cannot evaluate the content of the goal, AI is not able to identify potentially conflicting goals, such as when coachees want to work on their work-life balance while simultaneously striving to improve their job performance.

Box 15.1   AI, coaching, and bias

An extremely important point to be addressed as the use of AI in coaching continues to evolve is bias. The challenges with AI bias are relatively well documented (Williams, 2024) and refers to the occurrence of biased results due to human biases that skew the original data or AI algorithm (Holdsworth, 2023). AI bias is a serious issue and can significantly impact people's lives. For example, Williams (2024) explains how an AI system that is biased against certain racial or ethnic groups could deny them loans or jobs.

The potential bias in the programming of coachbots is even more likely when we consider that the coaching industry as a whole already contains huge amounts of bias. For example, Peake and Jones (2023) argue that there is an ingrained bias in both the research and practice of coaching, which means that the understanding of what influences coaching outcomes, particularly for marginalised groups, is severely lacking.

Therefore, as the use of AI in coaching continues to evolve, we must consider such questions as: Who is responsible for creating the algorithms used in coachbots and other AI coaching tools? And what level of representation do we have in these teams (e.g., gender, ethnicity, sexual orientation, cultural, disability, and other protected characteristics), to ensure that we are aware of potential biases, enabling us to take action to mitigate against them?

If coachbots are already in existence, what lies ahead in the future of coaching and AI? Perhaps the future of coaching practice in relation to AI may look a little like this:

- Foundational coaching functions (such as asking open questions to reflect on goals and formulating specific actions) may be replaced by AI-powered coachbots and there will be increased access to these so that almost everyone has access to a coachbot.

- This is likely to decrease the demand for coaching with human coaches, with coachbots replacing coaches who currently work at a foundational level, likely indicated by a lower hourly fee and often provided at scale through the digital coaching platforms (see Chapter 9 for a discussion of this) with coachees working in entry-level occupations or as individual contributors, rather than in leadership roles.
- However, the above will not replace human coaches entirely. Human coaching is likely to be reserved for coachees working in leadership or more complex roles who are faced with systemic, complex challenges, and who command higher salaries. (More on this in the next section).
- The use of AI to support human coaches in their practice may become more prevalent. For example, AI-generated insights and data analytics provided post-coaching session that can be used by the coach to enhance their practice and shared with the coachee to summarise key points, takeaways, actions, and refer on to helpful resources.

Box 15.2   The future of AI and democratising coaching

The rise in coaching provided by AI coachbots is often linked to the democratisation of coaching. For example, Passmore and Woodward (2023) argue that "AI solutions can operate at close to fixed cost, and thus truly democratise coaching by making it available for billions of users, instead of the millions who have the resource to access human to human conversations" (p. 13). However, whether AI coachbots will provide the solution to the lack of access to coaching will largely depend on how the coaching industry evolves. If our predictions come true, while a rise in AI coachbots will mean that more people will have access to coaching through coachbots than ever before, if human coaches are still utilised to complete the functions that AI coachbots cannot, this may serve to even further segment who has access to human coaches, as this will likely reduce the number of low-cost human coaches, driving up the price of human coaching even further.

Systemic approach to coaching

Our second prediction for the future of coaching builds on the first. The increase in the use of AI coachbots will likely mean that some functions of coaching can be easily and cost effectively replaced by AI. This will likely shift the focus of coaching provided by human coaches. Human coaches will need to fill the gap that AI cannot fill, and this is likely to be by taking a systemic approach to explore complex challenges (for more on systemic coaching, see Chapter 6).

O'Connor (2020) describes how working systemically helps us to understand interactions between components of a system, and how change in one aspect of a system can influence change in other aspects of the same system. Clutterbuck (2021) describes the essence of taking a systemic approach in coaching to viewing a situation or issue from multiple perspectives. "It's like walking round a complex structure and seeing it from different perspectives – from all four points of the compass, from above, from far above, and perhaps even from below" (Clutterbuck, 2021, p. 305). Components of a system can be anything from other people to events that have happened or are happening, to the historical, environmental, or social context, and to all the potential network of connections between these elements. Therefore, when we work systematically, we are considering much more in terms of what may be influencing the situation than in many other coaching approaches. Systemic coaching brings together the wider environmental and social context we live in; and by approaching challenges through this lens, we are enabled to see these challenges from a different perspective. Coaches will support coachees to elevate their mindset to systematic thinking (O'Connor, 2020), deepening their awareness of their role in affecting the system, connecting the dots as they navigate the more complex systematic forces that affect their teams, organisation, and industry.

This way of working is inherently far more complex and, as yet, AI is a very long way from being able to take a systemic approach to coaching, instead working in a more formulaic, linear way. When we consider working systemically as coaches, there are two other aspects that are helpful to consider in the context of the future of coaching practice. These are climate conscious coaching and equity, diversity, and inclusion in coaching.

Climate conscious coaching and equity, diversity, and inclusion in coaching

We are already seeing a recognition from many coaches that they, as individuals, and the coaching profession have a role to play in addressing big societal issues such as climate change and EDI. The perspective from these coaches is that it is not ethical to stand by and do nothing to address these issues when, through their coachees, they have access to decision makers who can have a significant impact on addressing climate change and EDI.

The Climate Coaching Alliance take this stance. The Climate Coaching Alliance state that their purpose is create a positive shift in human awareness to effect wider systemic changes in the world towards climate change and that they do this by influencing the global coaching community to bring the difficult questions of climate and ecological emergency into coaching conversations (Climate Coaching Alliance, 2024a). The Climate Coaching Alliance describe how their members work with a systemic mindset to support their coachees to engage more fully with the climate and ecological emergency, imagine possible futures, and do what is necessary to achieve them (Climate Coaching Alliance, 2024b).

In terms of equity, diversity, and inclusion, Roche and Passmore (2023) argue that there is a feeling among many coaches that there is "a gap, a silence, a blind spot in our profession when it comes to race" (p. 116). Shabi (2024) suggests that, increasingly, we are seeing coaches take a stand on diversity and inclusion; and Ayoade (2023) describes how coaching can assist coachees in better understanding the significance of diversity and inclusion, such as by recognising their biases, **prejudices**, and misconceptions, fostering personal growth and empathy.

Prejudice. A preconceived opinion or judgement about someone or something, often based on limited or biased information.

The critical point to consider with both climate conscious coaching and EDI in coaching, as explored in this context, is that **advocates** of these

Advocate. Individual or group that actively supports a cause, policy, or individual.

movements encourage coaches to bring these topics to the coaching conversation, even if the coachee has not suggested it. The argument here is that coaches have a responsibility and an ethical duty to shine a light on these important topics and raise awareness of the impact the coachee can have on these issues and, if we as coaches took this approach collectively, we would see an accelerated shift in progress on matters such as EDI and climate change. This approach, however, is of course a major shift from traditional models of coaching that emphasise that coaching is coachee-led and that the coaching agenda is dictated by the coachee. Perhaps, as AI coachbots replace some of the foundational coaching functions, the role of human coaches should become to ask the difficult questions that highlight the role each and every one of us has to play in taking responsibility and action in addressing the big challenges we all, as the human race, face.

Implications for the future of coaching education

There are potentially some key implications for coach education if the predictions we have outlined in this chapter for the future of coaching practice come to fruition:

- The rise in the use of digital tools in coaching will require much higher levels of **digital literacy** from coaches. To date, there are no such competencies in using technology in accepted coach competency frameworks (such as the ICF coaching competencies) and our anecdotal observations from working in the

> **Digital literacy.** The ability to effectively and critically use a range of digital technologies.

coaching industry are that there has not been widespread adoption of the use of digital coaching tools, despite most coaching taking place online and there being a range of excellent digital coaching tools already available. Therefore, the future of coaching education is likely to include a technical component where coaches are trained in how to use a wide variety of digital coaching tools, including enhancing their AI literacy (Li & Kim, 2024).

- If AI coachbots replace foundational coaching functions, human coaches will be required to engage in extended coach education to enable them to work effectively in more complex, systemic ways. This likely means that coach education organisations offering short courses will no longer be required and will need to be replaced by much more extensive training – for example, a full Master's in coaching may become the basic entry requirement to the coaching profession.

- If coaches are to become fluent in working systemically, they would need a deep foundational education in this approach, including their knowledge of matters such as climate change and EDI, to enable them to work confidently in these areas and add value beyond what a coachbot is able to offer. Currently, these matters, while covered in some coach education curriculums, do not appear to be considered core elements of a coach's education.

Implications for the future of the professionalisation of coaching

The potential changes to the practice of coaching described in this chapter would certainly also have implications for the professionalisation of coaching:

- With a growth in coachbots, ethical **codes of conduct** for the organisations responsible for the development and application of these coachbots would need to be put in

> **Code of conduct.** A set of guidelines that establishes expected behaviours, standards, and practices.

place, covering data security, bias, and managing emotionally charged situations (Diller, 2024).
- A shift in the focus and required level of competence for human coaches will have implications for competency frameworks. The reality for the coaching profession, if we are to see this change, is that there will be a decrease in the number of human coaches, as many foundational coaching tasks are replaced by coachbots and fewer human coaches work at a much more complex level.
- This may lead to a reduction in the number of coaching professional bodies. The current range of professional bodies is likely due, in part at least, to the high numbers of coaches. If the number of coaches reduces, so will the market size for the professional bodies.
- This may enable us to see a shift in the coaching industry to enable it to become more regulated, potentially following one accepted route to practise, similar to the route for practising occupational psychologists. This shift would certainly coincide with the requirement for more extensive foundational education.

Further reading and resources

The Coaching Psychology Pod. (2022, 1 March). How do coaches work race? (Series 1, Episode 4) [Audio podcast episode]. https://podcasts.apple.com/gb/podcast/how-do-coaches-work-race/id1608066740?i=1000552544052.

The Coaching Psychology Pod. (2022, 1 June). How is coaching changing for the future? (Series 1, E[isode 10) [Audio podcast episode]. https://podcasts.apple.com/gb/podcast/how-is-coaching-changing-for-the-future/id1608066740?i=1000564786618.

The Coaching Psychology Pod. (2024, 1 May). Our vision for the future: Where is the DoCP going? (Series 3, Episode 3) [Audio podcast episode]. https://podcasts.apple.com/gb/podcast/our-vision-for-the-future-where-is-the-docp-going/id1608066740?i=1000654139303.

References

Ayoade. A. (2023). The vital role of coaching in diversity, equity and inclusion. Accessed from https://www.forbes.com/sites/forbescoachescouncil/2023/11/29/the-vital-role-of-coaching-in-diversity-equity-and-inclusion/. Retrieved 8 June 2024.

Climate Coaching Alliance (2024a). Welcome to the climate coaching alliance. Accessed from https://www.climatecoachingalliance.org/. Retrieved 8 June 2024.

Climate Coaching Alliance (2024b). About CCA coaches. Accessed from https://www.climatecoachingalliance.org/background/about-cca-coaches/. Retrieved 8 June 2024.

Clutterbuck, D. (2021). Coaching teams positively from a complex, adaptive systems perspective. In W. A. Smith, I. Boniwell, & S. Green (eds), *Positive Psychology Coaching in the Workplace* (pp. 297–316). Springer.

Digital Tools (2024). What are digital tools. Accessed from https://www.walkme.com/glossary/digital-tools/. Retrieved 7 June 2024.

Diller, S. J. (2024). Ethics in digital and AI coaching. *Human Resource Development International, 27*(4), 584–596.

Graßmann, C., & Schermuly, C. C. (2021). Coaching with artificial intelligence: Concepts and capabilities. *Human Resource Development Review, 20*(1), 106–126.

Holdsworth, J. (2023). What is AI bias? Accessed from https://www.ibm.com/topics/ai-bias. Retrieved 7 June 2024.

ICF (2023). Global coaching study 2023 Executive summary. https://coachingfederation.org/app/uploads/2023/04/2023ICFGlobalCoachingStudy_ExecutiveSummary.pdf.

Li, H., & Kim, S. (2024). Developing AI literacy in HRD: Competencies, approaches, and implications. *Human Resource Development International*, 1–22.

Mai, V., Neef, C., & Richert, A. (2022). "Clicking vs. writing" – The impact of a chatbot's interaction method on the working alliance in AI-based coaching. *Coaching: Theorie & Praxis, 8*(1), 15–31.

O'Connor, S. (2020). Systemically integrated approaches to coaching: An introduction. *Philosophy of Coaching: An International Journal, 5*(2), 40–62.

Passmore, J., & Tee, D. (2023). The future is now: Digital coaching industry reviewed. *Coaching Today*, 47, 8–13.

Passmore, J., & Woodward, W. (2023). Coaching education: Wake up to the new digital and AI coaching revolution! *International Coaching Psychology Review*, 18(1), 58–72.

Peake, S., & Jones, R. J. (2023). The power of group coaching for women. Accessed from https://shapetalent.com/wp-content/uplo ads/2023/11/Shape-Talent-Group-Coaching-for-Women-White-paper.pdf. Retrieved 4 June 2024.

Roche, C., & Passmore, J. (2023). Anti-racism in coaching: A global call to action. *Coaching: An International Journal of Theory, Research and Practice*, 16(1), 115–132.

Shabi, A. (2024). How coaching has changed over the last 20 years. Accessed from https://www.linkedin.com/pulse/how-coaching-has-changed-over-last-hxrse/?trackingId=tPTxDcMZha2NsG8bpAc PXA%3D%3D. Retrieved 8 June 2024.

Williams, A. (2024). AI bias mitigation resources your whole team will love (technical and multidisciplinary). Accessed from https://www. holisticai.com/blog/technical-resources-bias-mitigation. Retrieved 7 June 2024.

Index

For Product Safety Concerns and Information please contact our EU
representative GPSR@taylorandfrancis.com
Taylor & Francis Verlag GmbH, Kaufingerstraße 24, 80331 München, Germany